THE VALU
INDUSTI
RELATIONS

Understanding Work and Employment Relations

Series Editors: **Andy Hodder**, University of Birmingham and **Stephen Mustchin**, University of Manchester

Published in association with the British Universities Industrial Relations Association (BUIRA), books in this series critically engage with issues of work and employment in their wider socio-economic context.

Also available in the series:

Forthcoming in the series:

Find out more at

bristoluniversitypress.co.uk/
understanding-work-and-employment-relations

THE VALUE
OF INDUSTRIAL
RELATIONS

Contemporary Work and
Employment in Britain

Edited by
Andy Hodder and Stephen Mustchin

BRISTOL
UNIVERSITY
PRESS

First published in Great Britain in 2024 by

Bristol University Press
University of Bristol
1–9 Old Park Hill
Bristol
BS2 8BB
UK
t: +44 (0)117 374 6645
e: bup-info@bristol.ac.uk

Details of international sales and distribution partners are available at bristoluniversitypress.co.uk

British Library Cataloguing in Publication Data
A catalogue record for this book is available from the British Library

ISBN 978-1-5292-3694-1 hardcover
ISBN 978-1-5292-3695-8 paperback
ISBN 978-1-5292-3696-5 ePub
ISBN 978-1-5292-3697-2 ePdf

Cover design: Nicky Borowiec
Front cover image: Vasyl / Adobestock
Bristol University Press uses environmentally responsible print partners.
Printed and bound in Great Britain by CPI Group (UK) Ltd, Croydon, CR0 4YY

FSC
www.fsc.org
MIX
Paper | Supporting
responsible forestry
FSC® C013604

Contents

Series Editors' Preface

Andy Hodder and Stephen Mustchin

We are very pleased to introduce the next volume in this book series, Understanding Work and Employment Relations. *The Value of Industrial Relations: Contemporary Work and Employment in Britain*, a multi-authored edited collection edited by series editors Andy Hodder and Stephen Mustchin, is the fourth text to be published in the series.

This series has been designed as a space for both monographs and edited volumes to highlight the latest research and commentary in the academic field of employment relations. The series is associated with the British Universities Industrial Relations Association (BUIRA), which marked 70 years of existence in 2020. The series seeks to draw on the expertise of the membership of BUIRA and contributions to its annual conference, as well as employment relations academics from around the world. Employment relations is a mature field of study and continues to be of relevance to academic and practitioner audiences alike. BUIRA recognizes the broad nature of the field of employment relations, and acknowledges that the field of study is constantly developing and evolving. BUIRA regards employment relations to be the study of the relation, control and governance of work and the employment relationship. It is the study of rules (both formal and informal) regarding job regulation and the 'reward–effort bargain'. These issues remain relevant today, in an era where the standard employment relationship has become increasingly fragmented due to employers' pursuit of labour flexibility, and we see the continued expansion of the gig or platform economy. Employment relations (and adjacent research areas including human resource management and the sociology of work) is taught widely in universities around the world, most commonly in business and management schools and departments. The field of study is multidisciplinary, encompassing law, politics, history, geography, sociology and economics. HRM has a tendency to focus uncritically on management objectives, without exploring issues of work and employment in their wider socio-economic context, and has its disciplinary roots in psychology, whereas employment relations retains a strong critical social science tradition. As scholars in this area, we feel that there is a need for regular, up-to-date, research-focused books that reflect current work in the field and go further than standard introductory texts. Through this book series, we aim to take an inter-disciplinary approach to understanding work and employment relations, and we welcome proposals from academics across this range of disciplines. We also welcome ideas and proposals from a broad range of international and comparative perspectives in order to reflect the increasingly diverse and internationalized nature of the field both in the UK and globally.

Published in collaboration with BUIRA, this book provides a critical review of the field of Industrial Relations (IR) and evaluates its future in the rapidly evolving world of work. Written by key authors in the field of IR, the book captures the significant transformations that have taken place within the subject area over the past decade. It traces the historical development of IR, exploring its ongoing impact on our lives. The chapters delve into various core aspects of IR, including union organization and mobilization, conflict at work, 'new' actors within IR, labour markets, management and HRM, IR theory, the role of the state, labour law, the influence of new technology and the examination of intersectionality in the context of work and employment.

We hope you enjoy reading this book. If you would like to discuss a proposal of your own, then email the series editors. We look forward to hearing from you.

Notes on Contributors

Ruth Dukes is Professor of Labour Law, University of Glasgow, UK.

Tony Dundon is Professor of Human Resource Management and Employment Relations, University of Limerick, Ireland.

Gregor Gall is Visiting Professor of Employment Relations, University of Leeds, UK.

Edmund Heery is Emeritus Professor of Employment Relations, Cardiff University, UK.

Andy Hodder is Reader in Employment Relations, University of Birmingham, UK.

Eleanor Kirk is Lecturer in Human Resource Management, University of Glasgow, UK.

Robert MacKenzie is Professor of Working Life Science, Karlstad University, Sweden.

Miguel Martínez Lucio is Professor of International Human Resource Management and Comparative Industrial Relations, University of Manchester, UK.

Anne McBride is Professor of Employment Studies, University of Manchester, UK.

Guglielmo Meardi is Professor of Sociology of Work and Economy, Scuola Normale Superiore, Italy.

Sian Moore is Professor of Employment Relations and Human Resource Management, University of Greenwich, UK.

Stephen Mustchin is Senior Lecturer in Employment Studies, University of Manchester, UK.

Kirsty Newsome is Professor of Employment Relations, University of Sheffield, UK.

Jenny K. Rodriguez is Senior Lecturer in Employment Studies, University of Manchester, UK.

Jill Rubery is Professor of Comparative Employment Systems, University of Manchester, UK.

Melanie Simms is Professor of Work and Employment, University of Glasgow, UK.

Adrian Wilkinson is Professor of Employment Relations, Griffith University, Australia, and University of Sheffield, UK.

Steve Williams is Reader in Employment Relations, University of Portsmouth, UK.

Stefanie Williamson is Research Associate, University of Sheffield, UK.

Introduction: The Enduring 'Point' and Value of Industrial Relations Research

Stephen Mustchin and Andy Hodder

Introduction

Industrial relations (IR) as a field of study principally focuses on the employment relationship and relations between workers and managers, subject matter that is of enduring interest and importance given the dominant role of waged labour in most people's lives (see Hodder and Martínez Lucio, 2021). Despite this, the field has frequently been framed in terms of crises and decline regarding its significance and relevance (see, for example, Strauss, 1989; Ackers and Wilkinson, 2008; Piore, 2011). Undoubtedly, the field has faced significant and ongoing challenges, including: the relative status and position of IR within increasingly marketized, neoliberal universities; the erosion of institutionalized IR, worker representation and collective bargaining within employing organizations; and the increasing influence on both academic and practitioner understandings of the employment relationship, which have to an extent shifted towards related fields of human resource management (HRM), organizational psychology, management studies (critical or otherwise) and similar.

In 2009, the British Universities Industrial Relations Association (BUIRA) published a landmark edited collection, provocatively titled *What's the Point of Industrial Relations* (Darlington, 2009), which was partly inspired by the dispute over the erosion and planned closure of the long-standing Centre for Industrial Relations at Keele University, where scholars in the field were pushed out of the institution, courses were marked for closure and management were evidently hostile towards, and did not value the field of, study (for an overview of the 2007–08 Keele dispute, see Lyddon, 2008;

Seifert, 2009). Featuring contributions from well-known academics in the field and adjacent subject areas, as well as important practitioner contributions from representatives of the Trades Union Congress (TUC) and the Advice, Conciliation and Arbitration Service (ACAS), the collection detailed the various challenges and attacks on the subject area while simultaneously highlighting the enduring academic and more practical importance and relevance of IR.

This book was initially conceived as a means of marking the 70-year anniversary of BUIRA in 2020 and as a follow-up to the 2009 collection. While this has been delayed by several years, in large part, due to the COVID-19 pandemic and the disruption it caused, the challenges identified in the 2009 collection have arguably worsened and intensified. This text, however, differs in focus from Darlington's edited collection. Rather than simply replicating and updating the 2009 text, in consultation with the BUIRA Executive Committee, we decided to take an alternative approach. We argue that IR as a field of study continues to endure and has to some extent seen some revival in terms of the richness of the subject matter addressed within IR research, writing and teaching, and the chapters brought together in this book highlight the enduring value of IR in a way that, despite the hostile environment within which IR scholars work, demonstrates its continuing importance, relevance and academic contribution.

We feel that there is a continuing value in producing edited collections of this type. From the 1970s until 2010, regular edited collections on the core subject matter of IR – the main actors within the employment relationship, for example, unions, management, the state and newer actors that influence the regulation of work; such processes as collective bargaining, pay determination and regulatory change; and such outcomes as the impact on labour markets, the nature of industrial conflict and similar – were produced by the long-established work of the Industrial – Relations Research Unit at Warwick University (Bain, 1983; Colling and Terry, 2010; Edwards, 1995, 2003), which were of great value both in terms of the intellectual foundations of IR research and as teaching materials. The last of these collections was published in 2010, and while excellent textbooks are still produced (for example, Farnham, 2015; Frege and Kelly, 2020; Williams, 2020; Bamber et al, 2021) and a number of very useful edited handbook collections have been produced in recent years (for example, Blyton et al, 2008; Gall, 2019), it was felt that there would be considerable value in producing a collection like this one with relatively concise overview chapters from key academics within the field of study of IR. This allows us to capture some of the significant changes within the field over the last decade or so, within which some major contributions have been made in terms of such issues as union organizing and mobilization, the impact of new technology, and the 'gig economy', as well as an increasing sensitivity to notions of intersectionality in terms of gender, race, migration, disability and related characteristics relevant to the study of work and employment. IR has evolved and been enriched in this period, as demonstrated by the range and breadth of subject matter presented at BUIRA conferences and other forums for the discussion and dissemination of IR research.

What do we mean by 'industrial relations'?

While we do not seek to restate well-rehearsed debates at any length, it is important to briefly outline what we consider to be the focus of the field of study. We believe that it is important to restate what we mean by 'industrial relations' and introduce the various contributions to this text. As outlined by BUIRA (2009: 47, emphases in original):

> the focus of industrial relations is on the regulation, control and – in the currently fashionable term – governance of work and the employment relationship. It is a *multi-disciplinary* (or, ideally, interdisciplinary) field of study, drawing on economics, law, sociology, psychology, political science and history. It provides a *multi-level* understanding of relationships at work, analysing the interconnections between the workplace, the company, the sector, the national regulatory framework and – increasingly – the European and global levels.

This quote highlights the breadth of IR, and it is important to note that this was written not as an attempt to broaden the field but to respond to attacks based on (often deliberate) misconceptions and, more positively, to explain the value of such an approach to the study of the employment relationship. The employment relationship has long been at the centre of IR, as evidenced by the opening statement of the *British Journal of Industrial Relations*, where the editors were at pains to point out that 'the focus of interest will be on the entire field of employment relationships and the environment in which they are shaped' (*BJIR*, 1963: 3; see also Kaufman, 2008). Although some in the past have suggested that a focus on the employment relationship is 'intellectually meaningless' (Strauss and Feuille, 1978: 275), it is now widely accepted that the starting point for understanding IR must be the employment relationship (see Edwards, 1995, 2003, 2005; Colling and Terry, 2010). We believe that this approach is necessary to contextualize the analysis of work relations in this manner and still holds value for the contemporary world of work, including those working in the gig economy.

The employment relationship is an exchange relationship and therefore a power relationship. It is also a social contract (Korczynski, 2023). The nature of the exchange between employer and employee is contradictory, exploitative and indeterminate. Central to this relationship are notions of power, politics and contest (Edwards, 2005). The wage–effort bargain:

> embraces the ways, both formal and informal, overt and tacit, in which workers and employers negotiate the terms of the labour contract. The terms of the bargain can never be wholly specified in advance, and just how much effort is put in for just what reward is determined daily (or even hourly). (Edwards and Hodder, 2022: 225)

There exists a 'structured antagonism' or a 'clash of interests' between capital and labour, which is at the heart of the employment relationship. In any employment relationship, 'workers are exploited in a very specific technical sense, namely, that they generate value in the labour process, and some of that value is taken from them' (Edwards, 2014: 12). Workers 'are subject to discipline, surveillance and control; the relevant systems of the employer structure the terrain on which the labour contract is negotiated' (Edwards and Hodder, 2022: 224). While the starting point for the study of IR is the employment relationship, it is important to remember that IR is a multi-level phenomenon and regulation can occur at local, sectoral, national and international levels, as businesses, labour and community organizations operate across borders, supply chains and online platforms (Wright et al, 2019).

As IR 'seeks to hold a mirror up to what goes on in the world of employment' (Sisson, 2010: 2), the approach adopted by IR scholars is of significant intellectual and practical importance. This is arguably as a result of the problem-centred orientation that has long dominated IR research and teaching (Kochan, 1998), and will not come as a surprise to those inside the field. As noted by BUIRA (2009: 53, 56): '[t]he agenda of industrial relations research and teaching thus has fundamental moral and practical importance ... [This] challenges students over questions that remain unaired elsewhere within the milieu of a business or management school.' We see this breadth as a positive characteristic of industrial relations, as it 'gives it an openness to a range of intellectual approaches and sensitivity to day-to-day realities' (Edwards, 2005: 267).

However, the nature of the field of study has meant that it has been criticized from various quarters (for a discussion of the challenges faced by IR research, see Edwards, 2005). A long-standing criticism levelled at IR has been the accusation that the field suffers from a lack of theory. These criticisms are often based on the idea that there should be one dominant theory in the field. However, 'the quest for a single unified theory of industrial relations is akin to being in a dark room and looking for a black cat that is not there' (Valizade, 2018: 688). We therefore follow Hyman (2004: 267), who stated: 'we certainly require theory in industrial relations, [but] it is neither possible nor desirable to pursue a self-contained theory of industrial relations'. Further criticism has come from researchers ensconced within HRM who have criticized IR for its supposed focus on collective bargaining and employment relationships in a context where such arrangements are in decline (Bratton and Gold, 2015). These authors suggest that IR has been 'eclipsed' by HRM and is thus no longer of relevance to understanding the contemporary world of work. However, such a view takes 'the easy way out' and is symptomatic of a growing trend whereby some academics feel the need 'to retreat into the comfort of our academic discipline, and within it, our favourite perspective' (Boxall, 2018: 27). While there is no need to repeat the long-standing debates between IR and HRM, many writers have suggested that both areas can coexist alongside one another (Boxall and Dowling, 1990: 204; Darlington, 2009), and an IR approach is of interest and use to scholars from cognate fields, such as sociology, economics, history, law and political science. There have also been a number of more radical critiques that have criticized the field as overwhelmingly Eurocentric, being situated within formalized notions of the employment relationship argued to be less relevant when considering the nature of labour within the 'Global South' (Nowak, 2021). Some of the criticism of IR, both from within and without the communities of scholars that constitute the field, are undoubtedly valid. A long-standing issue within the field has been insufficient attention to issues relating to what we now understand as intersectionality (see Greene, 2003; McBride et al, 2015; Rubery and Hebson, 2018; Lee and Tapia, 2021), and an overemphasis on (declining) institutional forms of employment regulation has arguably failed at times to capture the complex, changing nature of social relations within work, employment and society more generally. Such critiques are not new and are captured in Miliband's (1973: 73) criticism of IR as 'the consecrated euphemism for the permanent conflict … between capital and labour'. However, as noted by Hodder and Martínez Lucio (2021: 432): 'much work has been done to address these limitations, although such transitions are by no means complete'.

Drawing on the example of Britain alone, we would argue that many of the most significant developments, tensions and social changes of relevance to work and employment in recent years are central to the concerns and ongoing research within IR as a field of study. At the time of writing, these include: a cost-of-living crisis driven by inflation and exacerbated by pay suppression and austerity since the 2008 financial crisis (see Heyes et al, 2012; Williams and Scott, 2016); the prominence of issues during the COVID-19 pandemic relating to the inadequate regulation of workplace health and safety (Purkayastha et al, 2021); the transformation and degradation of work driven by new technology, and the dominance of tech multinationals (della Porta et al, 2022); the emergence of new, comparatively radical independent unions (Smith, 2022); the heightened state suppression of industrial action through legislation, including the Trade Union Act 2016 (Lyddon, 2021); the challenge to employment protections deriving from Brexit (Teague and Donaghey, 2018); the use of 'fire and rehire' tactics by significant numbers of employers (Bogg and Brodie, 2023); and the weakness of employment protections in the context of restructuring, as demonstrated by the example of the 2022 dismissal without consultation of 800 workers at the ferry company P&O (Dobbins, 2022). This book seeks to highlight this enduring relevance and the importance of IR in analysing, understanding and contributing to policy change, reform and collective action in terms of work and employment in a way that is lacking within competing fields that have sought to denigrate it for different reasons. While we focus on the UK in this text, we hope that readers from around the world will find this book to be of interest and relevance.

The book

It is of course impossible for one text, such as this, to coherently cover the full breadth and scope of matters relevant to the contemporary world of work and industrial relations. To do so would result in a very different (and much bigger) book. The chapters that follow this introduction complement each other in providing cogent, contemporary and innovative overviews of the theoretical and institutional context of IR as an academic field of study and the social relations within which it is located. In Chapter 2, Edmund Heery sets up the contributions that follow in his analysis of 'frames of reference' in the academic field of IR, including notions of interests within the employment relationship and analytical approaches informed by pluralist, unitary and radical frameworks, highlighting the movement of more unitary frames of reference into HRM and management studies, and the consolidation of more critical and radical framing within IR itself. In Chapter 3, Guglielmo Meardi builds on this by reflecting on theoretical framing and contributions within the field of IR, notably, system and stability theories and the importance of the role of crises within them. The lack of a 'grand theory' of IR is counterpoised with the significant existing and future theoretical contributions that IR can make to understandings of economic crisis, inequality and technological change. The theoretical themes within these introductory chapters are then followed by chapters analysing the main 'actors' within IR.

   In Chapter 4, Tony Dundon and Adrian Wilkinson bring the role of management into the framing of actors within the employment relationship. This chapter explores the nature of (analytical) HRM, its intertwined relationship with the field of IR and the importance of more critical, analytical approaches to HRM, with a focus on 'how people are managed at work and why they encounter certain employment experiences', as compared to more prescriptive, managerialist variants. Chapter 5, by Melanie Simms, evaluates the position of trade unions within the changing context of UK IR, covering the period from Thatcherism to more recent contextual changes in relation to financialization and the pandemic, along with reflections drawing on her long-standing contribution to debates on union organizing and renewal. In Chapter 6, Steve Williams highlights the emergence of 'new actors' within IR that play an increasingly significant role in the employment relationship and have historically been underexamined, including civil society organizations, law firms, employment agencies, employer forums and other bodies outside a traditional focus on employers, workers and unions, and the state. Miguel Martínez Lucio and Robert MacKenzie's Chapter 7 examines the role of the state within IR, an often underemphasized or at least narrowly defined social relationship deriving from governance institutions and systems of regulation, exploring sweeping yet contradictory transformations of the state under neoliberalism and themes of legitimacy, coordination and the marginalization of social and employment rights In Chapter 8, Jill Rubery explores the changing nature of labour markets and wider trends, including globalization, the dominance of the service sector, flexibilization and financialization, with reference to key recent developments in terms of technology, platform work and the pandemic, and the prospects for the further deterioration and segmentation of conditions of work.

In Chapter 9, Ruth Dukes and Eleanor Kirk explore the relationship between IR and labour law, subjects that have developed in silos to some extent in more recent decades but that clearly have a great deal to offer each other given their common focus on industrial justice, mobilization in relation to law and the legal and regulatory system, as well as the empirical contribution of IR to a more contextualized, sociological or socio-legal understanding of law in relation to work and employment. Their call for the 'recovery of a shared tradition' highlights these interrelationships and the subsequent scope for shared agendas in the future. Conflict at work and industrial action are the focus of Chapter 10 by Gregor Gall. These topics have arguably slipped down the agenda within IR in line with the wider decline in the incidence and extent of strikes in recent decades. These wider trends are considered in the context of the more recent, albeit limited, upsurge of industrial action since 2022 in Britain and elsewhere, as well as the enduring importance of 'examining whether the means are available to workers to express the conflict they are subject to and part of'. In Chapter 11, Sian Moore, Kirsty Newsome and Stefanie Williamson focus on new technology and the role of online platforms in terms of their impact on work and IR. Themes of flexibility, work autonomy, digital technology and self-employment are explored, with a highly illustrative case study of parcel delivery, highlighting the relationship between such 'flexible' work, labour market segregation and inequality. The final contribution, Anne McBride and Jenny Rodriguez's Chapter 12, analyses the relationship between the field of IR and intersectionality. They argue that intersectionality – a focus on the influence of, and interrelationship between, gender, 'race', class and other characteristics – is underdeveloped in IR research and call for greater sensitivity within the field to such structural inequalities, how they intersect and their relevance for the study of the employment relationship.

We hope that the chapters in this volume show that the field of IR continues to have a promising future. In this chapter, we have outlined the role that an IR approach has to play in understanding the world of work. We have acknowledged some of the challenges and criticisms levelled at IR research, but believe that there is a need to be optimistic about the future of the field of study. The COVID-19 pandemic illustrated the resilience of IR research and the continued value of such an approach as IR issues became central to public concern (see Hodder and Martínez Lucio, 2021). The recent wave of strike action has continued to demonstrate that this increased interest in IR matters needs to be maintained, both in the UK and beyond (see Kochan et al, 2023). The challenge for us all is to ensure that IR does not stand still but, rather, continues to evolve and expand in order to maintain an interest in understanding the politics of work.

References

Ackers, P. and Wilkinson, A. (2008) 'Industrial relations and the social sciences', in P. Blyton, N. Bacon, J. Fiorito and E. Heery (eds) *The Sage Handbook of Industrial Relations*, London: Sage, pp 53–68.

Bain, G.S. (ed) (1983) *Industrial Relations in Britain*, London: Blackwell.

Bamber, G., Cooke, F.L., Doellgast, V. and Wright, C.F. (eds) (2021) *International and Comparative Employment Relations*, 7th edn, London: Sage.

BJIR (*British Journal of Industrial Relations*) (1963) 'Introductory note', *British Journal of Industrial Relations*, 1(1): 3–4.

Blyton, P., Bacon, N., Fiorito, J. and Heery, E. (eds) (2008) *The Sage Handbook of Industrial Relations*, London: Sage.

Bogg, A. and Brodie, D. (2023) 'Every little helps: permanent benefits, contract interpretation, and "fire and rehire"', *Industrial Law Journal*, 52(1): 246–72.

Boxall, P. (2018) 'The development of strategic HRM: reflections on a 30-year journey', *Labour and Industry*, 28(1): 21–30.

Boxall, P. and Dowling, P. (1990) 'Human resource management and the industrial relations tradition', *Labour and Industry*, 3(2–3): 195–214.

Bratton, J. and Gold, J. (2015) 'Towards critical human resource management education (CHRME): a sociological imagination approach', *Work, Employment and Society*, 29(3): 496–507.

BUIRA (British Universities Industrial Relations Association) (2009) 'What's the point of industrial relations?', in R. Darlington (ed) *What's the Point of Industrial Relations? In Defence of Critical Social Science*, Salford: BUIRA, pp 46–59.

Colling, T. and Terry, M. (eds) (2010) *Industrial Relations: Theory and Practice*, 3rd edn, London: John Wiley & Sons.

Darlington, R. (ed) (2009) *What's the Point of Industrial Relations? In Defence of Critical Social Science*, Salford: BUIRA.

Della Porta, D., Chesta, R.E. and Cini, L. (2022) *Labour Conflicts in the Digital Age: A Comparative Perspective*, Bristol: Bristol University Press.

Dobbins, T. (2022) 'The "wicked problem" behind P&O Ferries sackings', Birmingham Business School Blog, University of Birmingham. Available at: https://blog.bham.ac.uk/business-school/2022/04/05/the-wicked-problem-behind-po-ferries-sackings/

Edwards, P. (ed) (1995) *Industrial Relations: Theory and Practice*, London: John Wiley & Sons.

Edwards, P. (ed) (2003) *Industrial Relations: Theory and Practice*, 2nd edn, London: John Wiley & Sons.

Edwards, P. (2005) 'The challenging but promising future of industrial relations: developing theory and method in context-sensitive research', *Industrial Relations Journal*, 36(4): 262–82.

Edwards, P. (2014) Warwick Papers in Industrial Relations Number 99, Warwick University. Available at: https://warwick.ac.uk/fac/soc/wbs/research/irru/publications/warwickpapers_industrialrelations/wpir_110.pdf

Edwards, P. and Hodder, A. (2022) 'Conflict and control in the contemporary workplace: structured antagonism revisited', *Industrial Relations Journal*, 53(3): 220–40.

Farnham, D. (2015) *The Changing Faces of Employment Relations: Global, Comparative and Theoretical Perspectives*, London: Palgrave Macmillan.

Frege, C. and Kelly, J. (eds) (2020) *Comparative Employment Relations in the Global Economy*, 2nd edn, London: Routledge.

Gall, G. (ed) (2019) *Handbook of the Politics of Labour, Work and Employment*, Cheltenham: Edward Elgar.

Greene, A.-M. (2003) 'Women and industrial relations', in P. Ackers and A. Wilkinson (eds) *Understanding Work and Employment*, Oxford: Oxford University Press, pp 305–15.

Heyes, J., Lewis, P. and Clark, I. (2012) 'Varieties of capitalism, neoliberalism and the economic crisis of 2008–?', *Industrial Relations Journal*, 43(3): 222–41.

Hodder, A. and Martínez Lucio, M. (2021) 'Pandemics, politics, and the resilience of employment relations research', *Labour & Industry*, 31(4): 430–8.

Hyman, R. (2004) 'Is industrial relations theory always ethnocentric?', in B. Kaufman (ed) *Theoretical Perspectives on Work and the Employment Relationship*, Urbana-Champaign: IIRA, pp 265–92.

Kaufman, B. (2008) 'Paradigms in industrial relations: original, modern and versions in-between', *British Journal of Industrial Relations*, 46(2): 314–39.

Kochan, T. (1998) 'What is distinctive about industrial relations research?', in K. Whitfield and G. Strauss (eds) *Researching the World of Work*, Ithaca, NY: ILR Press, pp 31–45.

Kochan, T., Fine, J., Bronfenbrenner, K., Naidu, S., Barnes, J., Diaz-Linhart, Y., Kallas, J., Kim, J., Minster, A., Tong, D., Townsend, P. and Twiss, D. (2023) 'An overview of US workers' current organizing efforts and collective actions', *Work and Occupations*, 50(3): 335–50.

Korczynski, M. (2023) 'The social contract of work: moving beyond the psychological contract', *Human Resource Management Journal*, 33(1): 115–28.

Lee, T. and Tapia, M. (2021) 'Confronting race and other social identity erasures: the case for critical industrial relations theory', *Industrial and Labor Relations Review*, 74(3): 637–62.

Lyddon, D. (2008) 'Editorial: the dispute at Keele', *Historical Studies in Industrial Relations*, 25–26: vii–xiv.

Lyddon, D. (2021) 'Strike ballots under the 2016 Trade Union Act: unions mobilise to counter the latest legal onslaught', *Industrial Relations Journal*, 52(6): 479–501.

McBride, A., Hebson, G. and Holgate, J. (2015) 'Intersectionality: are we taking enough notice in the field of work and employment relations?', *Work, Employment and Society*, 29(2): 331–41.

Miliband, R. (1973) *The State in Capitalist Society*, London: Quartet.

Nowak, J. (2021) 'From industrial relations research to global labour studies: moving labour research beyond Eurocentrism', *Globalizations*, 18(8): 1335–48.

Piore, M. (2011) 'Whither industrial relations: does it have a future in post-industrial society?', *British Journal of Industrial Relations*, 49(4): 792–801.

Purkayastha, D., Vanroelen, C., Bircan, T., Vantyghem, M.A. and Gantelet Adsera, C. (2021) *Work, Health and Covid-19*, Brussels: European Trade Union Institute.

Rubery, J. and Hebson, G. (2018) 'Applying a gender lens to employment relations: revitalisation, resistance and risks', *Journal of Industrial Relations*, 60(3): 414–36.

Seifert, R. (2009) 'Industrial relations at Keele University: in the end it is always political!', in R. Darlington (ed) *What's the Point of Industrial Relations*, Salford: BUIRA, pp 68–76.

Sisson, K. (2010) 'Employment relations matters'. Available at: https://warwick.ac.uk/fac/soc/wbs/research/irru/publications/erm/apreface.pdf

Smith, H. (2022) 'The "indie unions" and the UK labour movement: towards a community of practice', *Economic and Industrial Democracy*, 43(3): 1369–90.

Strauss, G. (1989) 'Industrial relations as an academic field: what's wrong with it?', in J. Barbash and K. Barbash (eds) *Theories and Concepts in Comparative Industrial Relations*, Columbia, SC: University of South Carolina Press, pp 241–60.

Strauss, G. and Feuille, P. (1978) 'Industrial relations research: a critical analysis', *Industrial Relations*, 17(3): 259–77.

Teague, P. and Donaghey, J. (2018) 'Brexit: EU social policy and the UK employment model', *Industrial Relations Journal*, 49(5–6): 512–33.

Valizade, D. (2018) 'Book review: *A New Theory of Industrial Relations: People, Markets and Organizations after Neoliberalism*, by Conor Cradden', *British Journal of Industrial Relations*, 56(3): 686–8.

Williams, S. (2020) *Introducing Employment Relations: A Critical Approach*, 5th edn, Oxford: Oxford University Press.

Williams, S. and Scott, P. (eds) (2016) *Employment Relations under Coalition Government: The UK Experience, 2010–2015*, London: Routledge.

Wright, C., Wood, A., Trevor, J., McLaughlin, C., Huang, W., Harney, B., Geelan, T., Colfer, B., Chang, C. and Brown, W. (2019) 'Towards a new web of rules: an international review of institutional experimentation to strengthen employment protections', *Employee Relations*, 41(2): 313–30.

2

Frames of Reference
in Industrial Relations

Edmund Heery

Introduction

Since it was first introduced by Alan Fox in the 1960s, 'frames of reference' has been an enduring concept within the field of industrial relations. It refers to the broad interpretations of the nature of the employment relationship held either by actors in the real world of industrial relations – workers, employers and policy makers – or by academic commentators. In his first use of the term, Fox (1966) drew a distinction between a unitary frame of reference – grounded in the belief that the employment relationship was essentially cooperative and that employers and employees shared common interests whose advance was best secured through the exercise of management prerogative – and a pluralist frame, which recognized that conflict was integral to the employment relationship and that, as a consequence, employees needed independent representation through trade unions and collective bargaining to safeguard their separate interests. In a later formulation, Fox identified a third, radical frame, which emphasized the exploitative nature of employment within capitalist societies and was critical of the pluralist perspective for promoting employee accommodation with this prevailing system (Fox, 1974).

In the period since Fox was writing, researchers have continued to use the frame concept both to analyse the beliefs of industrial relations actors and to identify and reflect upon competing traditions within the academic field (Heery, 2016; Budd et al, 2021; Dobbins et al, 2021; Kaufman et al, 2021). Later writers have often labelled frames differently and have sometimes identified more frames than the three sketched by Fox, but they share his concern to identify broad perspectives on the employment relationship that include both analytical and normative claims grounded in very different assumptions about the relative interests of workers and their employers (Budd and Bhave, 2008; Godard, 2017; Barry and Wilkinson, 2021). In what follows, there is an attempt to demonstrate the continuing relevance of the frame concept and to show how unitary, pluralist and radical/critical perspectives remain identifiable within the academic field of industrial relations.

Frames of reference

Frames of reference are rooted in competing interpretations of the relative interests of employers and workers, and can be placed on a continuum along which the interests of the two sides are fully congruent at one end and absolutely conflicting at the other. In what follows, the guiding assumptions about the relative interests of employers and workers of the unitary, pluralist and critical frames are set out before considering several other analytical dimensions on which the three frames differ. These dimensions comprise the identification of pressing labour problems, prescriptions for solving these problems, the theoretical explanations that are typical of the different frames and the social actors to which they assign decisive, agentic capacity.

Relative interests

In the unitary frame, the interests of employers and workers are viewed as congruent: the two sides possess distinct interests in the realm of employment – their interests are not identical – which can be advanced simultaneously through a single course of action. For example, it has been argued that the adoption of a living wage can enable the 'capability' of employees, allowing them to lead less constrained lives, while also solving problems of labour supply and performance for employers (Werner and Lim, 2016; Werner, 2021). This congruence of interests tends to be theorized in one of two ways by adherents to the unitary frame. On the one hand, it can have a basis in psychology, whereby employers offer employees work that is meaningful, satisfying, engaging or developmental, which, in turn, reinforces positive attitudes and behaviours for the employer, such as commitment, citizenship, motivation and high performance. On the other hand, congruence can be effected through an economic mechanism in which incentives are used to align the interests of principals (employers) and agents (workers). These incentives may assume an immediate form, as through payment by results, but they can also offer deferred benefits to employees through internal labour markets, seniority systems, share options and occupational pensions, which serve to motivate loyalty and skills acquisition. The psychological variant of unitarism underpins a great deal of contemporary human resource management (HRM) scholarship, while the economic version is seen in its purest form in personnel economics (Lazear and Gibbs, 2009; Boxall and Purcell, 2015).

The critical interpretation of interests is at the opposite end of the continuum to that of the unitary frame and assumes that employers and workers have sharply opposed interests. This belief is often associated with another: that conditions for employees are undergoing a fresh process of degradation that extends across multiple types of work, multiple industries and multiple locations. Degradation, in turn, is typically grounded in a theory of capitalist development in which each stage generates new forms of immiseration. The most widespread version of this argument is encapsulated by the concept of 'neoliberalism': the belief that the global economy entered a new phase of development in the 1980s marked by, among other things, more intensive forms of labour exploitation. The era of neoliberalism, critical scholars argue, is characterized by more precarious work, new forms of workplace surveillance and the 'fissuring' of organizations through outsourcing, deregulation and de-unionization (Baccaro and Howell, 2017; Milkman, 2020). These long-run trends, moreover, have been intensified since the imposition of austerity in the wake of the 2008 financial crisis (Dundon et al, 2020).

The pluralist conception of relative interests sits between these two extremes. Pluralists accept that workers have separate and opposed interests to those of employers, and believe that institutions are required to protect workers' separate interests because, in most cases, workers have less power than employers. These institutions can collectivize workers and represent their interests, as trade unions do, or they can regulate employer behaviour, as employment law does, thereby limiting the capacity of employers to enforce the kind of degradation of work identified by critical scholars. Pluralist assumptions about relative interests also contain other elements. While opposed interests are identified, the gap between them is not seen as irreconcilable, and pluralists uniformly are supportive of collective bargaining, through which unions and employers negotiate temporary accords that resolve disputes and formulate agreements that both sides can accept. Another assumption is that the degree of conflict of interests varies by issue and that while distributive questions concerning wage rates and similar matters are highly conflictual, other matters, such as investment and skill development, may allow for the identification of 'mutual gains' (Kochan and Osterman, 1994). For pluralists, there are shared as well as conflicting interests in the employment relationship, which can provide the basis for labour–management partnership. A final assumption is that this zone of common interests can be expanded through public policy. For pluralists, the function of regulation is typically to impose 'beneficial constraints' on employers that make adversarial approaches to management costly and induce businesses to cooperate with their employees (Streeck, 1997).[1]

Labour problems

According to Kaufman (1993: 4), the field of industrial relations emerged in response to the 'labor problem', that is, the growth of the organized industrial working class in the late 19th century, and since its emergence, the field has continued to be preoccupied with addressing successive labour problems. The three frames of reference have tended to conceive of labour problems in different ways. For unitarists of an economic stamp, labour market institutions have often been identified as the source of labour problems because they distort market forces and make it impossible to align the economic interests of employers and employees. On this view, trade union bargaining power and legal regulation often generate perverse effects for workers, discouraging investment, depressing wage growth or generating unemployment, contrary to their ostensible purposes (see Heery, 2011). More typically among unitary scholars, however, labour problems are regarded as arising from 'management failure'. One of the main themes in unitary writing on work of the past 15 years has been the need to generate greater employee engagement at work (Alfes et al, 2010). This perceived need arises from survey evidence that many employees are disengaged from work, thereby imposing a brake on business performance. The main identified source of this disengagement is management failure; toxic leaders, poor managers, work systems that limit autonomy and human resource systems that fail to develop employees lie behind the epidemic of disengagement. On this view, if there is a labour problem, then it is one of employers' own making.

For pluralists, in contrast, labour problems are often believed to arise from 'market failure' (Wright, 2023). A paradigmatic example of this argument can be seen in the case of low pay. In poorly regulated markets, from which unions are largely excluded and in which the statutory minimum wage is either inadequate or poorly enforced, employers will be able to exercise monopsony power to drive wages down (Manning, 2003). The results of this imbalance in the employment relationship are low pay, in-work poverty, rising inequality and a broad swathe of other social and economic problems that stem from low earnings. Critical writers share the concern of pluralists to identify the adverse consequences for workers of the contemporary economic system, though, as we have seen, diagnosis extends beyond specific cases of market failure to encompass the broadest features of capitalist development. Other aspects of critical discussion of the labour problem include: an overwhelming focus on problems *for* labour and uninterest in questions of economic performance and social integration; an increasing preoccupation with the precarity of much employment, which has been added to a long-standing concern with the dehumanizing and controlling aspects of work (Dundon et al, 2020); and a desire to capture the lived experiences of employees trapped in exploitative work through ethnography and other qualitative methods. The series of 'On the Front Line' articles in the journal *Work, Employment and Society*, which report testimony from the contemporary workplace, exemplifies this last approach.

While identifying the problems for labour inherent in neoliberalism is one approach to the labour problem within the critical frame, another is to focus on the 'problem of resistance'. Countermovements are necessary to challenge the prevailing order, and it is believed that only through conflict and mobilization will the separate interests of workers be advanced. A great deal of critical scholarship within industrial relations is therefore aimed at identifying countermovements, assessing their potential and analysing the conditions that either retard their growth or facilitate their emergence. There is now a vast international literature on 'union renewal', which starts from a critique of the failings of the established labour movement and identifies new strategies that have the capacity to mount a major challenge to capital (Luce, 2014; Holgate, 2021; see also Chapter 5). Recent contributions have focused on community unionism, the revival of traditional militancy and the activities of new, indie unions organizing among the precariat (Connolly and Darlington, 2012; Holgate, 2015; Peró, 2019). Much of this work is prefigurative, reporting on small-scale developments that are believed to have the potential to escalate into powerful movements of resistance. The risk in this strategy, however, is that many of these developments may remain marginal, or outliers, rather than the wave of the future.

Prescription

Frames of reference have normative as well as analytical components, and their adherents have not only identified labour problems but also offered prescriptions for their solution. For writers in the unitary tradition, the default prescription is that employers must manage better. Better management might take the form of adopting a particular technique or standard. It might also take the form of adopting a bundle of reinforcing HR practices that have been shown to be associated with high performance or of developing an HR system that flows from and reinforces wider business strategy (Baron and Kreps, 1999; Procter, 2008). There is an active debate within the field of HRM about which techniques or combination of techniques are most effective in aligning employer and employee interests, as well as different interpretations about how they generate their positive effects (Boxall and Purcell, 2015). What unites the competing positions, however, is the central unitary claim that the separate interests of employers and employees can be and are best advanced by unilateral management decision making.

For pluralists, the default prescription has been for better regulation, such that management decision making is constrained and channelled along paths that require accommodation with employee interests. When Fox was writing, the primary form of regulation advocated by pluralists was collective bargaining, and pluralist schemes for the reform of industrial relations continue to recommend legal and policy changes that can support bargaining. One contrast with the reform agenda with which Fox was associated in the 1960s, however, is a contemporary focus on multi-employer industry bargaining rather than bargaining at the workplace level. The Institute of Employment Rights has formulated a comprehensive programme for rebuilding multi-employer bargaining in the UK, much of which has been adopted by the Labour Party (Ewing et al, 2020).

Another change in pluralist prescription since Fox, however, has been greater advocacy of other forms of regulation. As unions and collective bargaining have declined in the UK, so pluralists have looked to employment law as a means of regulating employer behaviour. A particular emphasis in recent years has been placed on the need for stronger regulation of precarious forms of employment, such as gig work and zero-hours contracts (Taylor et al, 2017). In addition, pluralists have called for strengthening the means of legal enforcement, arguing that the existing, largely complaint-driven system should be supplemented with wider legal duties for employers to adhere to labour standards and for the UK to establish the kind of general labour inspectorate seen in other countries (Dickens, 2012; Sisson, 2016). Pluralist prescription has also extended beyond law. Increasingly, pluralists have argued for the reform of corporate governance and modes of corporate financing from a belief that prevailing forms, which prioritize shareholder value, at best, inhibit and, at worst, undermine cooperative approaches to industrial relations (Sisson, 2016; 2020).

The prescription offered by critical scholars has also altered since Fox's time. In the 1960s and 1970s, critical scholarship was preoccupied with the shop-steward movement and its potential to mount a fundamental challenge to the prevailing industrial order. Researchers assessed workplace militancy, factory occupations, combine committees, alternative workers' plans and worker cooperatives (Coates and Topham, 1988). Since these heady days, the labour movement has suffered prolonged decline, and the attention of the critical frame has switched, as we have seen, to the issue of union renewal. There are perhaps three main overlapping currents in this body of more recent work. A syndicalist current has focused on how unions can rebuild and deploy their internal sources of strength through organizing and mobilizing (see Heery, 2015). A second current has examined attempts to supplement the powers of unions through alliances with other social movements, what Gumbrell-McCormick and Hyman (2013) have called 'coalitional power resources'. The final current has considered union responses to the changing composition of the workforce, with notable recent contributions assessing union representation of migrant and precarious workers (Doellgast et al, 2018; Milkman, 2020; Holgate, 2021). The focus of attention of the critical frame has altered over time, therefore, but the broad thrust of prescription, that is, identifying effective countermovements to the power of employers, has remained constant.

Explanation

Critical writers have tended to pitch their explanations of developments in industrial relations at a deep, structural level, identifying long-run trends in the capitalist economy that drive common employer approaches to management across multiple contexts. Institutional differences between regions and nations are played down in this approach to analysis, while structural forces themselves are often divided into stages, such as neoliberalism, or conceived of in terms of a single transformative variable, such as financialization or rentierism (Baccaro and Howell, 2017). Each phase or each transformative force is associated with its own forms of labour immiseration and creates the terrain on which countermovements emerge (Bailey et al, 2021). Indeed, a central concept for many critical writers is that capitalist development is contradictory, calling forth resistance to counter the particular forms of work degradation to which phases give rise (Harvey et al, 2018). There is also often a punctuated quality to the explanatory models that underpin critical analysis, with an attempt to identify periods of flux when capital becomes vulnerable to challenge, countermovements are most likely to emerge and radical change has most chance of being achieved (Kelly, 1998). Within critical analysis, crisis is inherent to the development of capitalism and provides a window of opportunity to those whose interest lies in challenging the existing order.

In both the psychological and economic variants of unitarism, theoretical explanation has often focused on modelling the response of individual employees to the deployment of management techniques. In work psychology, the 'AMO' framework has been influential, which attributes the positive effects of HRM to the degree to which employees have the ability (A), motivation (M) and opportunity (O) to perform at a high level (Boxall and Purcell, 2015). Lying beneath modelling of this kind, however, are often more general claims about the evolution of post-industrial societies, which are believed to select for forms of management that align worker and employer interests, and which are the mirror image of the types of explanation favoured by critical writers. In some versions, these selective pressures stem from product markets, in which quality and customer responsiveness have become determinants of competitive success, and that require motivated and engaged employees to provide necessary levels of service (see Korczynski, 2002). Other versions of the argument attribute selective pressure to new technologies that require higher levels of skill and the exercise of discretion, or to the changing composition of the workforce, which has become more reflexive and demanding of greater autonomy in working life. Whatever the precise causal mechanism identified, however, unitary scholars, like their critical counterparts, tend to claim that long-term, structural changes in the economy and society underpin their prescriptions for progressive forms of management.

At the time when Fox was writing, pluralists also made use of this kind of argument. The emergence of an industrial relations system based on trade union representation and collective bargaining was viewed as an integral feature of a mature industrial society, characteristic of all developed economies (Kerr et al, 1955). In the period since, this belief has become less tenable, as union membership and collective bargaining have shrunk in coverage across most advanced capitalist countries. Pluralists now tend to favour institutional explanations of industrial relations, drawn from the broader fields of socio-economics and political economy. For example, Heery et al's (2020) study of the living wage in the constituent countries of Great Britain is informed by the work of social geographers and regional economists who have identified the 'unbundling' of national political systems and an expanding role for regional and city governments (see also Ayres et al, 2018). Other pluralists have drawn heavily on socio–economic literature in the 'varieties of capitalism' tradition, which explains national differences in industrial relations in terms of the competing dynamics of 'liberal' and 'coordinated' forms of political economy (Hall and Soskice, 2001). It has become routine for assessments of employer behaviour, public policy, collective bargaining and labour market outcomes in the UK to attribute these to the fact that the country is a 'liberal market economy' (see Dundon et al, 2014). It is partly for this reason that pluralist prescription for reform has extended outwards beyond the bounds of industrial relations, as traditionally conceived, to encompass issues of corporate governance and finance. It is only by reconfiguring the basic institutional structure of British capitalism that a more just, balanced and productive settlement will be achieved in the sphere of employment.

Agency

As well as offering different types of structural explanation of industrial relations, writers from the three frames have tended to attribute decisive agency to different social actors. For those from the unitary frame, employers possess decisive agency, generating labour problems through mismanagement and resolving those problems by adopting techniques, bundles or strategies that realign employer and employee interests. Reflecting the priority accorded to employers, unitary writers tend to downplay the potential of government to bring about decisive change in industrial relations. Unitary advocates of diversity management, for instance, have argued that legislative action to promote equality and diversity at work has limited effect, likely only to elicit resistance or minimal compliance from employers. What is needed instead is culture change within management, supported by demonstrating that there is a strong business case for managing diversity (Kandola, 2009).

For pluralists, this set of assumptions is reversed. While positive action by employers to tackle labour problems is welcomed, it is argued that action of this kind is likely to be confined to those businesses that can identify a clear business rationale or that can afford to introduce positive changes at minimum cost. Reliance on voluntary action by employers will leave those businesses untouched that are not persuaded of the business case for equality and diversity, or other good labour standards, or that actively benefit from exploitative labour practices (Dickens, 1999). It is for this reason that most pluralists identify the state as the decisive social actor, capable of instituting fundamental change in the system of industrial relations. As we have noted, pluralists attribute many contemporary problems to market failure and to the institutional features of the UK's political economy. Tackling problems with deep-seated causes of this kind is believed to be beyond the capacities of private actors and can only be dealt with meaningfully through public policy. When Fox was writing, many pluralists adhered to a voluntarist position in industrial relations, in which state action was kept to a minimum and the regulation of the labour market was trusted to the independent action of trade unions and employers through 'free collective bargaining'. This faith in voluntarism is less apparent within pluralist writing today, and state action is usually identified as the decisive means for effecting industrial relations reform (see Heery, 2011).

There is a Janus-like quality to critical perceptions of agency. On the one hand, critical writers have often emphasized the decisive agency of capital in imposing new forms of work degradation. Thus, Wood (2020) has characterized the workplace regime in the burgeoning service economy as one of 'flexible despotism' and identified the potential for 'algorithmic control' through gig-economy platforms that capture customer ratings of worker performance. On the other hand, critical writers attribute agency to workers themselves in developing resistance to capital and to each new phase of exploitation; indeed, Wood has also mapped new forms of resistance within service work that use social media both to create networks among employees and to impose reputational costs on employers by exposing malpractice. For critical writers in industrial relations, the countermovement of workers drives progressive change, limiting management control and compelling employers to comply with labour standards. Countermovements may only emerge in specific conjunctures and exert decisive influence for limited periods, but they are viewed as essential, endowing the evolution of industrial relations with a cyclical rhythm of control and resistance. There is a dialectical quality to industrial relations for the critical frame, in which the agency of workers plays a decisive part (Bailey et al, 2021).

Conclusion

The three frames of reference identified by Fox 50 years ago continue to shape writing about work today, and the frame concept retains its utility as a means of identifying the competing positions within the field of industrial relations. There have been changes in the relative standing of the three frames since Fox was writing, however. For Fox, unitary thinking was largely located beyond the academy among employers and establishment commentators – in Fox's (2004) autobiography, he references a pamphlet by the late Duke of Edinburgh as an example of the latter. In the period since, the unitary frame has colonized much academic writing on work, not among scholars who identify with the field of industrial relations but in adjacent fields beyond, such as HRM, occupational psychology, personnel economics and business ethics. In Fox's time, non-union, paternalist businesses like the John Lewis Partnership were viewed as an idiosyncratic survival from an earlier age; now, they are regarded as repositories of best practice (Salaman and Storey, 2016).[2]

The other frame whose fortunes have waxed since Fox first identified it is the critical frame. Critical writing on industrial relations, sometimes labelled 'critical labour studies', is arguably now dominant and the primary perspective presented in such influential journals as *Work, Employment and Society*. There is something paradoxical about this development because it has occurred despite the decline of the labour movement and the transfer of most industrial relations scholarship to business schools. The fear has often been expressed that the latter shift would herald the demise of critical research on work and employment, but this has not been realized to date. Critical industrial relations has seemingly found a secure niche within UK business education.

The frame of reference whose fortunes have waned is the pluralist frame. Pluralists very much occupied the industrial relations mainstream in the 1960s and 1970s, but in the period since, they have lost out to their unitary and critical counterparts. Pluralist writers have seen much of their earlier access to the makers of public policy disappear, and their prescriptions for reform have fallen out of favour, notwithstanding a limited revival under the New Labour governments of Blair and Brown, and continuing receptiveness within the devolved governments of Scotland and Wales. The pluralist frame *has* suffered from the decline of the labour movement. In the face of this decline in influence over public policy, the pluralist frame has been pulled in two opposing directions. On the one hand, pluralists have turned to HRM, and many of the leading lights of the latter began their careers as industrial relations pluralists. On the other hand, pluralists have moved closer to the critical wing, focusing on problems *for* labour and developing a critique of the UK's weakly regulated and poorly performing system of industrial relations (Sisson, 2020; Wright, 2023). As much public policy has shifted in the direction of neoliberalism, so has conventional pluralism, with its support for trade unionism, collective bargaining and the effective regulation of employer behaviour to import balance into the employment relationship, become a critical frame of reference itself.

Notes

[1] Focusing on the relative interests of workers and employers neglects the fact that women and members of minority groups have separate interests at work to those of men and majority groups. One response to the recognition of diverse interests among employees within the literature on frames has been to identify distinct feminist and race-based perspectives on work (Budd and Bhave, 2008). An alternative is to retain the trinity of unitary, pluralist and critical frames but examine how each has responded to the recognition of multiple sex- and identity-based interests that fracture the traditional category of 'worker' (Heery, 2016).

[2] That said, John Lewis has struggled financially post-COVID-19 (Butler, 2023) due to higher financial costs compared to many competitors.

References

Alfes, K., Truss, C., Soane, E., Rees, C. and Gatenby, M. (2010) *Creating an Engaged Workforce*, London: Chartered Institute of Personnel and Development.

Ayres, S., Flinders, M. and Sandford, M. (2018) 'Territory, power and statecraft: understanding English devolution', *Regional Studies*, 52(6): 853–64.

Baccaro, L. and Howell, C. (2017) *Trajectories of Neoliberal Transformation: European Industrial Relations since the 1970s*, Cambridge: Cambridge University Press.

Bailey, D.J., Lewis, P. and Shibata, S. (2021) 'Contesting neoliberalism: mapping the terrain of social conflict', *Capital and Class*, 46(3): 449–78.

Baron, R. and Kreps, D. (1999) *Strategic Human Resources: Frameworks for General Managers*, New York: Wiley.

Barry, M. and Wilkinson, A. (2021) 'Old frames and new lenses: frames of reference revisited', *Journal of Industrial Relations*, 63(2): 114–25.

Boxall, P. and Purcell, J. (2015) *Strategy and Human Resource Management*, 4th edn, Basingstoke: Palgrave MacMillan.

Budd, J.W. and Bhave, D. (2008) 'Values, ideologies, and frames of reference in industrial relations', in P. Blyton, N. Bacon, J. Fiorito and E. Heery (eds) *The Sage Handbook of Industrial Relations*, London: Sage Publications, pp 92–112.

Budd, J.W., Pohler, D. and Huang, W. (2021) 'Making sense of (mis)matched frames of reference: a dynamic cognitive theory of (in)stability in HR practices', *Industrial Relations*, 61(3): 268–89.

Butler, S. (2023) 'Five reasons why John Lewis and Waitrose are having a tough year', *The Guardian*, 4 March. Available at: www.theguardian.com/business/2023/mar/04/five-reasons-why-john-lewis-and-waitrose-are-having-a-tough-year

Coates, K. and Topham, T. (1988) *Trade Unions in Britain*, 3rd edn, London: Fontana.

Connolly, H. and Darlington, R. (2012) 'Radical political unionism in France and Britain: a comparative study of Sud-Rail and the RMT', *European Journal of Industrial Relations*, 18(3): 235–50.

Dickens, L. (1999) 'Beyond the business case: a three-pronged approach to equality action', *Human Resource Management Journal*, 9(1): 9–19.

Dickens, L. (2012) 'Fairer workplaces: making employment rights effective', in L. Dickens (ed) *Making Employment Rights Effective: Issues of Enforcement and Compliance*, Oxford and Portland, OR: Hart Publishing, pp 205–28.

Dobbins, T., Hughes, E. and Dundon, T. (2021) 'Zones of contention in industrial relations: framing pluralism as praxis', *Journal of Industrial Relations*, 63(2): 149–76.

Doellgast, V., Lillie, N. and Pulignano, V. (2018) 'From dualization to solidarity: halting the cycle of precarity', in V. Doellgast, N. Lillie and V. Pulignano (eds) *Reconstructing Solidarity: Labour Unions, Precarious Work, and the Politics of Institutional Change in Europe*, Oxford: Oxford University Press, pp 1–41.

Dundon, T., Dobbins, T., Cullinane, N., Hickland, E. and Donaghey, J. (2014) 'Employer occupation of regulatory space of the Employee Involvement and Consultation (I&C) Directive in liberal market economies', *Work, Employment and Society*, 28(1): 21–39.

Dundon, T., Martínez Lucio, M., Hughes, E., Howcroft, D., Keizer, A. and Walden, R. (2020) *Power, Politics, and Influence at Work*, Manchester: Manchester University Press.

Ewing, K., Hendy, J. and Jones, C. (2020) *A Manifesto for Labour Law*, 2nd edn, London: Institute for Employment Rights.

Fox, A. (1966) *Industrial Sociology and Industrial Relations*, Royal Commission on Trade Unions and Employers' Associations, Research Paper 3, London: Her Majesty's Stationery Office.

Fox, A. (1974) *Beyond Contract: Work, Power and Trust Relations*, London: Faber & Faber.

Fox, A. (2004) *A Very Late Development: An Autobiography*, 2nd edn, Keele: British Universities Industrial Relations Association.

Godard, J. (2017) *Industrial Relations, the Economy, and Society*, 5th edn, Concord, Ontario: Captus Press.

Gumbrell-McCormick, R. and Hyman, R. (2013) *Trade Unions in Western Europe: Hard Times, Hard Choices*, Oxford: Oxford University Press.

Hall, P.A. and Soskice, D. (eds) (2001) *Varieties of Capitalism: The Institutional Foundations of Comparative Advantage*, Oxford: Oxford University Press.

Harvey, G., Turnbull, P. and Wintersberger, D. (2018) 'Speaking of contradiction', *Work, Employment and Society*, 33(4): 719–30.

Heery, E. (2011) 'Debating employment law: responses to juridification', in P. Blyton, E. Heery and P. Turnbull (eds) *Reassessing the Employment Relationship*, Basingstoke: Palgrave, pp 342–71.

Heery, E. (2015) 'Unions and the organizing turn: reflections after 20 years of Organizing Works', *The Economic and Labour Relations Review*, 26(4): 545–60.

Heery, E. (2016) *Framing Work: Unitary, Pluralist, and Critical Perspectives in the Twenty-First Century*, Oxford: Oxford University Press.

Heery, E., Hann, D. and Nash, D. (2020) 'Political devolution and employment relations in Great Britain: the case of the Living Wage', *Industrial Relations Journal*, 51(5): 391–409.

Holgate, J. (2015) 'An international study of trade union involvement in community organizing: same model, different outcomes', *British Journal of Industrial Relations*, 53(2): 460–83.

Holgate, J. (2021) *Arise: Power, Strategy, and Union Resurgence*, London: Pluto Press.

Kandola, R. (2009) *The Value of Difference: Eliminating Bias in Organizations*, Oxford: Pearn Kandola Publishing.

Kaufman, B.E. (1993) *The Origins and Evolution of the Field of Industrial Relations in the United States*, Ithaca, NY: Cornell University Press.

Kaufman, B.E., Barry, M., Wilkinson, A., Lomas, G. and Gomez, R. (2021) 'Using unitarist, pluralist and radical frames to map the cross-section distribution of employment relations practices across workplaces: a four country empirical investigation of patterns and determinants', *Journal of Industrial Relations*, 63(2): 204–34.

Kelly, J. (1998) *Rethinking Industrial Relations: Mobilization, Collectivism, and Long Waves*, London: Routledge.

Kerr, C., Dunlop, J.T., Harbison, F. and Myers, C. (1955) *Industrialism and Industrial Man*, Cambridge, MA: Harvard University Press.

Kochan, T.A. and Osterman, P. (1994) *The Mutual Gains Enterprise*, Boston, MA: Harvard University Press.

Korczynski, M. (2002) *Human Resource Management in Service Work*, Basingstoke: Palgrave.

Lazear, E. and Gibbs, M. (2009) *Personnel Economics in Practice*, 2n edn, Hoboken, NJ: John Wiley and Sons.

Luce, S. (2014) *Labor Movements: Global Perspectives*, Cambridge: Polity Press.

Manning, A. (2003) *Monopsony in Motion: Imperfect Competition in Labour Markets*, Princeton, NJ: Princeton University Press.

Milkman, R. (2020) *Immigrant Labor and the New Precariat*, Cambridge: Polity Press.

Peró, D. (2019) 'Indie unions, organizing and labour renewal: learning from precarious migrant workers', *Work, Employment and Society*, 34(5): 900–18.

Procter, S. (2008) 'New forms of work and the high performance paradigm', in P. Blyton, N. Bacon, J. Fiorito and E. Heery (eds) *The Sage Handbook of Industrial Relations*, London: Sage, pp 149–69.

Salaman, G. and Storey, J. (2016) *A Better Way of Doing Business? Lessons from the John Lewis Partnership*, Oxford: Oxford University Press.

Sisson, K. (2016) *Shaping the World of Work – Time for a UK Jobs Strategy*, Warwick Papers in Industrial Relations, Number 105, Coventry: Industrial Relations Research Unit, University of Warwick.

Sisson, K. (2020) *Making Britain the Best Place to Work: How to Protect and Enhance Workers' Rights after Brexit … and Coronavirus*, Warwick Papers in Industrial Relations, Number 111, Coventry: Industrial Relations Research Unit, University of Warwick.

Streeck, W. (1997) 'Beneficial constraints: on the economic limits of rational voluntarism', in J. Rogers Hollingsworth and R. Boyer (eds) *Contemporary Capitalism: The Embeddedness of Institutions*, Cambridge: Cambridge University Press, pp 197–218.

Taylor, M., Marsh, G., Nichol, D. and Broadbrent, P. (2017) *Good Work: The Taylor Review of Modern Working Practices*, London: Department of Business, Energy, and Industrial Strategy.

Werner, A. (2021) 'Why do managers of small and medium-sized businesses seek voluntary Living Wage accreditation? An exploration of choice rationales', *European Journal of Work and Organizational Psychology*, 30(6): 778–89.

Werner, A. and Lim, M. (2016) 'The ethics of the living wage: a review and research agenda', *Journal of Business Ethics*, 137: 433–47.

Wood, A.J. (2020) *Despotism on Demand: How Power Operates in the Flexible Workplace*, Ithaca, NY, and London: ILR Press.

Wright, C.F. (2023) 'Addressing problems *for* labour not problems *of* labour: the need for a paradigm shift in work and industrial relations policy', *Labour and Industry*, 33(1): 11–21.

3

Capitalist Crises and Industrial Relations Theorizing

Guglielmo Meardi

Introduction

The field of industrial relations does not have a unified grand theory, and attempts to build it have never had a lasting success. As a social science field of study, it draws on theoretical paradigms from different disciplines to frame theoretical statements on the meanings, causes and effects of the processes it studies. The frequent statement that it suffers from atheoretical empiricism is unwarranted: theoretical articles and books are among the most cited in industrial relations journals, yet theory in industrial relations often remains implicit.

This reflection takes the form of a journey through the main theoretical contributions that have appeared on the idea of crisis as the focal point of the 'labour problem' notion at the centre of the field of industrial relations. The *raison d'être* of industrial relations comes from the indeterminacy and antagonism inherent to the employment relationship, which make existing disciplines (economics, psychology, law and so on) unable to fully conceptualize it. The 'labour problem' has emerged most sharply in the phenomenon of 'crisis', not only as a social crisis of order and inequality but also as a political and economic crisis. Not all industrial relations theorizing is directly about crisis, but even that about order exists in the shadow of the possibility or memory of crisis, as in the idea that a functioning industrial relations system should regulate industrial conflict in a well-ordered way. This journey will therefore follow the various crises of capitalism as the milestones of theoretical reflection about work.

Economic crisis and industrial relations theory

The history of capitalism has been a history of crises, even if some extended periods of growth, such as the Fordist/Keynesian postwar decades, had given the impression that the risk of crisis had been forever removed. From the beginning, as can be seen in Marx's works between the 1850s and 1860s,[1] it has been difficult to distinguish between (cyclical) 'capitalist crises' and 'the capitalist crisis'. Following, approximately, the Kondratieff waves, the most remarkable financial crises in the capitalist era have been those of 1847, 1893, 1929, 1973 and 2008 – followed by the 'exogenous' crisis of 2020. All of these moments have marked social thought about work, at the same time as they led to deep political change.

The 1847 financial panic (itself fuelled by trade disruptions starting with the 1845 potato famine in Ireland) indirectly prepared the political ground for the *Communist Manifesto* the year after and, more directly, started Marx's political-economy reflection on crisis that culminated in the theory of the falling rate of profit. That reflection became the pillar of one of the most important theoretical approaches, or frames of reference, of industrial relations. However, while it was centred on the nexus between capital and labour, it was indeed before 'industrial relations' as a term, and before industrial relations developed into a field focusing on the institutions and processes that explain the dynamic of the employment relationship.

That term and that field of inquiry were born of the following major international financial crisis in 1893. Sydney and Beatrice Webb published their *History of Trade Unionism* (Webb and Webb, 1894) the year after and *Industrial Democracy* in 1897 (Webb and Webb, 1897), starting the tradition of scientific analysis of collective worker organization. However, the 1893–97 crisis also fuelled interest in a totally different contribution about work, Pope Leo XIII's *Rerum Novarum* encyclical ([1891] 1990), which become the building block of Catholic social teaching. It was with a study of *Rerum Novarum* that the young John Commons (1894) inaugurated his interest in the politics of work. That interest soon met the emerging institutional theory of Thorstein Veblen, leading to the foundation of the industrial relations field in the US. With Commons' (1905) *Trade Unionism and Labor Problems*, the expression 'labour problem' became the field's centre of attention. On the other side of the Atlantic in those same years, Emile Durkheim and Max Weber developed parallel reflections on the rules and institutions of capitalism, which laid the theoretical foundations for economic sociology and then, respectively, the functionalist and institutionalist approaches in industrial relations. These theoretical developments were parallel to deep political change. The social discontent across Europe in the last decade of the 19th century marked the development of labour movements, including the cementing of 'new

27

unionism' in Britain, and of their political wings, from the Labour Party (founded in 1890) to revisionist social-democracy (Eduard Bernstein published the *Probleme des Sozialismus* articles in 1896–98).

The 1929 crash and the Great Recession were a further critical seizure. The political impact included the New Deal and the National Labor Relations Act 1935 in the US, the Fronts Populaires in Europe, and, last but not least, the rise of fascism. Thinking about capitalism and work unavoidably asked for big theories: all was at stake in the works of Schumpeter, Keynes, Polanyi and, from his constrained prisoner viewpoint, Gramsci. Keynesianism started from the problem of the crisis and would go on to frame employment policies for decades. On a parallel path, Michał Kalecki theorized the role of unemployment as a discipline mechanism. Polanyi took the institutionalist and Marxist critiques of the commodification of labour to another level with his theory of embeddedness, still central today to new economic sociology and theories of labour power (Burawoy, 1979; Silver, 2003). That focus on big issues meant that in most advanced countries, the 1930s were not conducive to elaborations on industrial relations in the narrow sense. Even in the US and UK, despite important policy developments, the original academic field started to decline. Commons' last important work, *Institutional Economics* of 1934, was an attempt to go beyond industrial relations to build a broader institutional theory.

After the Second World War 2 and the so-called '*trente glorieuses*', the issue of economic crisis hit the capitalist world again in 1973 after the collapse of Bretton Wood and the oil shock, starting a political-economy shift away from the Fordist compromise and Keynesianism. The 1970s became an extremely fertile period of renewal in industrial relations thinking, focusing on the crisis while also affected by the experience of the 1960s' new social movements. The dominant pluralist and systemic approaches were challenged, on one side, by the 'radical' frame of reference, which adapted Marxist concepts to contemporary capitalism (Hyman, 1975), and, on the other – mostly in Continental Europe – by the corporatist school (Schmitter, 1974; Crouch, 1977) and the *école de la régulation* (Aglietta, 1976). The 1970s saw the pioneering comparative studies of trade union renewal and mobilizations (Crouch and Pizzorno, 1978), as well as the first systematic considerations of the role of the state in industrial relations (Crouch, 1982). Among these works were the first feminist contributions linking crisis, work and gender (Milkman, 1976). The feminization of employment (coinciding, in the 1970s, with male-dominated sectors' initial decline) was accompanied by a growing presence of women in a hitherto almost entirely male field of studies and of feminist contributions (Cook, 1980) in a mostly gender-blind scholarship. Both female scholars and feminist theory would deeply change the field in the following decades by redefining its central object: work.

The latest major capitalist economic crisis occurred in 2008–09. Its political and institutional effects are still to be assessed but included a new

Eurogovernance system in the European Union and the rise of nationalist populism in both advanced and emerging economies, which required industrial relations to develop new analytical tools and more attention to the transnational dimension (Erne, 2015). Some important industrial relations theorists reacted with a 'radical turn'. This is visible in recent works by Crouch (2011) and Streeck (2016), previously associated with corporatist and institutional theories, who have adopted more critical standpoints towards neoliberalism and capitalism. It is also expressed by the growing criticism of the varieties of capitalism approach (Hall and Soskice, 2001) and the rediscovery of theories stemming from the previous crises, such as those of Kalecki and of the *école de la régulation* (Baccaro and Howell, 2017). Another way in which the 2008–09 crisis marked theories about work was by revealing the depth of labour market precarization, even in the 'coordinated market economies' that had been associated with employment security, resulting in new concepts like the 'precariat', as distinct from the 'salariat' that traditional industrial relations had focused on (Standing, 2011).

From this historical overview, it emerges how for the broad field of industrial relations, periods of crisis have been times to focus on the 'big issues' of labour under capitalism and to borrow from the broader social sciences – sociology, economics, political science and so on. That does not mean that industrial relations theory advances only through crises, as the periods in between have seen equally important advances, but the difference in focus is striking. Applying the important distinction proposed by Heery (2008) between system and change theories, the approaches focusing on the former were dominant in periods of stability, while, as reported earlier, in periods of crisis, those of change gained traction. The 1910s and 1920s were the beginning of the institutionalization of industrial relations as a distinct field in the US (and to a lesser extent in the UK). The post-war growth decades were those when Dunlop's (1958) system theory of industrial relations dominated in the US, the pluralist approach of the Oxford school dominated in the UK and Walton and McKersie (1965) developed the behaviour theory of labour negotiations. In all these cases, industrial relations were largely insulated from (in Dunlop's case, as a subsystem of) the broader capitalist context.

The years of prevailing stability and optimism between 1989 and the 2008 crisis were equally a time for 'system' theories, as well as for micro approaches. The 'varieties of capitalism' approach (Hall and Soskice, 2001), with its institutional complementarities argument to explain stability and path dependency, became extremely popular in comparative debates. As put by Baccaro and Howell (2017) in their critique, the varieties of capitalism theory privileged second-order geographic variation over macro-level, dialectic and dynamic historical variation, or, as put by labour process theorists, it spends 'too much time on the variety and not enough on the capitalism' (Thompson, 2010: 12).

There is no reason why 'crisis' theories should be intrinsically deeper or more robust than the 'system' ones, or vice versa. One could say, in an arch-materialist way, that the dialectic between the two corresponds to the structural dialectic of capitalism itself. However, at a time when industrial relations as a field is in many ways shrinking institutionally and questioned academically, times of crisis have provided fertile encounters with broader theories. Furthermore, as has been argued from different standpoints (Kaufman, 2008; Meardi, 2014), the future of the field has more promising prospects if recentred on the broad notion of 'labour problems' than if narrowed down to the micro level of the employment relationship, where the 'imperialistic' competition between human resources management, psychology and behavioural science over the last four decades has left less space for industrial relations approaches than there was in the 1950–80 period.

What industrial relations tells us about crises

If industrial relations theory has learnt a lot from periods of crisis, what have we learnt about crises from industrial relations research? In other words, if it is easy to make an argument for industrial relations openness to, and cross-contamination with, broader social theories, it has become less simple to make a case for the importance of industrial relations for the social sciences. Yet, industrial relations research on periods of crisis has produced a body of knowledge that is relevant not just within its own field. Extracting from a complex and variegated literature, this knowledge can be summarized as a theory of labour movements as quasi-cyclical, which helps to address questions on social stability that arise in any economic crisis.

This theory is based on four pillars of research: strikes, trade union membership, collective bargaining and tripartism. Research on strikes – which was more popular when strike statistics produced higher total numbers than in recent years – has indicated a double effect of crises on industrial action (Franzosi, 1995). The first is negative, via unemployment, which tends to scare workers off and reduce union power by putting them on the defensive; however, the second can be positive if the crisis is associated with inflation (as happened in the 1920s and 1970s but notably not after 2008), as with inflation, wage increases become more important in relation to the costs of industrial action. A separate argument that can be seen as corollary of this is that strikes are more frequent in the 'transition periods' between upswings and downswings in the long economic Kondratieff waves (Kelly, 1997). In Kelly's argument, such periods were the early 1870s, the early 1990s, the post-First World War and post-Second World War periods, and 1967–75, with the qualification that the effect on strikes can be mitigated by corporatist institutions. Recently, Kelly (2018) had to qualify this argument to explain why no wave of strikes occurred around the latest economic turning points.

A similar argument has been made by studies of trade union membership, which appears to be cyclical and helped by low unemployment and inflation (Schnabel, 2013). As with strikes, institutional factors mitigate these effects in some countries by changing the logic of unionization, but the association remains well established, with the caveat that it is about absolute numbers rather than the rate of unionization: in case of rapid rises of unemployment, the unionization rate can actually grow if, as often happens, including in the most recent economic crisis, job losses are disproportionately concentrated among non-members.

As to collective bargaining, the evidence is less clear-cut: the 1929 one had a positive effect (and arguably already the 1893 one), but it was the opposite for the 1973 one (Brown, 1983). A post-2008 crisis review stressed the role of state policies in explaining the heterogeneous effects of crises on collective bargaining (Brandl and Traxler, 2011), and a more recent analysis of the 2010s sees complex forms of hybridization (Brandl and Bechter, 2019). In the European context, the complexity of the latest economic crisis is closely linked to changes in Eurogovernance, a field that industrial relations has contributed to dissect (Erne, 2015; Höpner and Lutter, 2018). Finally, the relationship between cyclical crises and tripartite governance has been most elegantly put in the 'corporatist Sisyphus' argument by Schmitter and Grote (1997), which complements the long-wave one by Kelly on strikes: times of crisis disrupt previous settlements while preparing the demand for new concertation.

Taken together, these contributions have an important cautionary lesson for the fields of political economy and social movement studies. Recurrent expectations that crisis leads to working-class social protest are misplaced, as they ignore the specific dynamics of labour power resources. More conducive times for labour advances are, in fact, the periods just before, for example, when growth starts slowing down (Kelly, 1997). In terms of policy, however, crises are moments of innovation, as they open up opportunities for change, which can easily take the form of social protection and wage coordination in closed economies but in more liberal international settings, as in the financial and monetary crisis of 2008–10, is more likely to involve decentralization and liberalization.

The theoretical challenge of the pandemic crisis

Writing during the pandemic crisis makes it impossible to assess its industrial relations implications, as it would have been writing in 1929, 1973 or 2008. Yet, the different nature of a crisis that is exogenous to capitalism (though not to globalization) is worth underlining. The pandemic caused a crisis that was not so much of demand (as typically in capitalist crises) but rather of supply: the sudden limitations to the possibility of mobilizing the labour force. This difference makes the crisis more ambiguous in terms of employment and negotiation power between employers and employees. While the unemployment rate has hardly increased in most advanced countries, the activity rate has plummeted, and a large number of workers are furloughed. As a result, governments and employers have faced new challenges that require both concessions and listening to workers. In a number of countries, such as France, Denmark and Italy, national and sectoral agreements on health and safety and on remote working were quickly signed, as governments did not have the expertise or the legitimacy to impose radical work restructuring (Meardi and Tassinari, 2022). In social and employment policy, the flexibilization trend of the last few decades was reversed, with priority given to employment protection. In some cases, major policy innovation occurred, as with the furlough scheme in the UK, in striking contrast with the refusal (by a Labour government) to consider short-working-hour schemes in 2008–09. This trend appeared to continue with the labour shortages reported in many countries at the beginning of the recovery.

The second major difference is the role of discursive and ethical dimensions on a crisis that is around a social value like health more than about economic interests. Some recent works in industrial relations have pointed at discursive power and symbolic politics (Chun, 2011; Sallaz, 2019). This aspect is very visible in new discourses around the definition of 'key workers' during the pandemic, and whether the new discourses about essential work, the value of care work and the balance between work and life will affect the power balance in industrial relations is of major theoretical relevance. Ethical and symbolic politics provide opportunities, but like all power resources, they need to be mobilized by agency, and variation in their extent and form is to be considered. The concomitant return of inflation, as in the past, has contributed to a resurgence of industrial action.

Finally, the pandemic is widely associated with a halt to globalization or even the beginning of deglobalization. It is premature to predict what will follow, as well as in consideration of the war in Ukraine. However, the state has already proved capable of taking radical decisions about the economy, about borders and about individual freedoms that the 'retreat of the state' discourse of the 1990s–2000s thought impossible. The precedent will stay and may feed the already previously visible trend towards more state governance of employment relations (Meardi, 2018).

Conclusion

The contradictory nature of employment relations, involving both control and consent, as well as conflict and cooperation, benefits from both crisis and stability theorizing. Strong crisis theories also have to consider how crises are, at least temporarily, overcome – as done by the *école de la regulation*, corporatist theory, Keynesian and Polanyian approaches. Symmetrically, system and stability theories need to contemplate the idea of crisis: in a dynamic system like employment under capitalism, all compromises, governance methods and psychological contracts contain the seeds of their own contestation.

It is not surprising, therefore, that during the recent crises, we have seen more calls for theoretical renewal, as well as for a return to the classics, which are still considered classic because they did not take capitalism for granted. Such calls have come from theoretical books (for example, Heery, 2016; Cradden, 2017), special issues in journals like *Industrial and Labor Relations Review* (Volume 74, Issue 3, 2021) and the *Journal of Industrial Relations* (Volume 63, Issue 2, 2021), and reactions against the 'psychologization' of industrial relations (Godard, 2014; Budd, 2020; Kaufman, 2020).

This return to theory is not simple, as the financialization of the economy has questioned the centrality of work in the economy that was evident at the peak of industrial society. A grand theory of industrial relations as an autonomous field is not practicable in the context of the geographic, demographic, technological and political diversification of employment. However, industrial relations scholarship has made some strong contributions to the understanding of the financial crisis, as with the idea of 'privatized Keynesianism' (Crouch, 2009). It also keeps contributing to the understanding of central socio-economic problems, such as inequality (even if the link between collective bargaining and equality is increasingly ambiguous) and technology (even if the public debates tend to prefer more extreme, technological-determinist voices). All this points to the need for industrial relations to think big.

Note

[1] In 1850, fresh from the 1847–48 economic and political turmoil, Marx and Engels (1978: 264) wrote: 'whereas hitherto every crisis has been the signal for further progress, for new victories by the industrial bourgeoisie over the landowners and financial bourgeoisie, this crisis will mark the beginning of the modern English revolution'. By 1864–65, writing what would become the third book of *Capital*, Marx was much more cautious and concentrated on the theory of crisis at the more abstract level of the system's logic rather than on the chronicle of historically specific crises.

References

Aglietta, M. (1976) *A Theory of Capitalist Regulation: The US Experience*, London: Verso.

Baccaro, L. and Howell, C. (2017) *Trajectories of Neoliberal Transformation*, Cambridge: Cambridge University Press.

Brandl, B. and Bechter, B. (2019) 'The hybridization of national collective bargaining systems: the impact of the economic crisis on the transformation of collective bargaining in the European Union', *Economic and Industrial Democracy*, 40(3): 469–89.

Brandl, B. and Traxler, F. (2011) 'Labour relations, economic governance and the crisis: turning the tide again?', *Labor History*, 52(1): 1–22.

Brown, W. (1983) 'The impact of high unemployment on bargaining structure', *Journal of Industrial Relations*, 25(2): 132–9.

Budd, J.W. (2020) 'The psychologisation of employment relations, alternative models of the employment relationship, and the OB turn', *Human Resource Management Journal*, 30(1): 73–83.

Burawoy, M. (1979) *Manufacturing Consent: Changes in the Labor Process under Monopoly Capitalism*, Chicago, IL: University of Chicago Press.

Chun, J.J. (2011) *Organizing at the Margins: The Symbolic Politics of Labor in South Korea and the United States*, Ithaca, NY: Cornell University Press.

Commons, J. (1894) *Social Reform and the Church*, New York: Crowell.

Commons, J. (1905) *Trade Unionism and Labor Problems*, Boston, MA: Ginn & Company.

Commons, J. (1934) *Institutional Economics: Its Place in Political Economy*, New York: Macmillan.

Cook, A. (1980) *The Most Difficult Revolution: Women and Trade Unions*, Ithaca, NY: Cornell University Press.

Cradden, C. (2017) *A New Theory of Industrial Relations*, London: Routledge.

Crouch, C. (1977) *Class Conflict and the Industrial Relations Crisis*, London: Heinemann.

Crouch, C. (1982) *The Politics of Industrial Relations*, London: Fontana.

Crouch, C. (2009) Privatised Keynesianism: an unacknowledged policy regime, *The British Journal of Politics and International Relations*, 11(3): 382–99.

Crouch, C. (2011) *The Strange Non-death of Neoliberalism*, Cambridge: Polity.

Crouch, C. and Pizzorno, A. (eds) (1978) *Resurgence of Class Conflict in Western Europe since 1968*, London: Palgrave.

Dunlop, J. (1958) *Industrial Relations Systems*, New York: Holt.

Erne, R. (2015) A supranational regime that nationalizes social conflict, *Labor History*, 56(3): 345–68.

Franzosi, R. (1995) *The Puzzle of Strikes: Class and State Strategies in Postwar Italy*, Cambridge: Cambridge University Press.

Godard, J. (2014) 'The psychologization of employment relations?', *Human Resource Management Journal*, 24: 1–18.

Hall, P. and Soskice, D. (eds) (2001) *Varieties of Capitalism*, Oxford: Oxford University Press.

Heery, E. (2008) System and change in industrial relations analysis, in P. Blyton et al (eds) *The SAGE Handbook of Industrial Relations*, London: Sage, pp 69–91.

Heery, E. (2016) *Framing Work: Unitary, Pluralist and Critical Perspectives in the Twenty-First Century*, Oxford: Oxford University Press.

Höpner, M. and Lutter, M. (2018) 'The diversity of wage regimes: why the Eurozone is too heterogeneous for the Euro', *European Political Science Review*, 10(1): 71–96.

Hyman, R. (1975) *Industrial Relations. A Marxist Introduction*, London: Palgrave.

Kaufman, B. (2008) 'Paradigms in industrial relations: original, modern and versions in-between', *British Journal of Industrial Relations*, 46(2): 314–39.

Kaufman, B. (2020) 'The real problem: the deadly combination of psychologisation, scientism, and normative promotionalism takes strategic human resource management down a 30-year dead end', *Human Resource Management Journal*, 30(1): 49–72.

Kelly, J. (1997) 'Long waves in industrial relations: mobilization and counter-mobilization in historical perspective', *Historical Studies in Industrial Relations*, 4(1): 3–35.

Kelly, J. (2018) 'Rethinking industrial relations revisited', *Economic and Industrial Democracy*, 39(4): 701–9.

Leo XIII [1891] (1900) *Rerum Novarum: de conditione opificum*, transl. Leo XIII (2019) *Rerum Novarum: Encyclical of Pope Leo XIII on Capital and Labor*. Available at: https://www.vatican.va/content/leo-xiii/en/encyclicals/documents/hf_l-xiii_enc_15051891_rerum-novarum.html

Marx, K. and Engels, F. (1978) *Collected Works*, Vol 10, London: Lawrence & Wishart.

Meardi, G. (2014) 'The (claimed) growing irrelevance of employment relations', *Journal of Industrial Relations*, 56(4): 594–605.

Meardi, G. (2018) 'Economic integration and state responses: change in European industrial relations since Maastricht', *British Journal of Industrial Relations*, 56(3): 631–55.

Meardi, G. and Tassinari, A. (2022) 'Crisis corporatism 2.0? The role of social dialogue in the pandemic crisis in Europe', *Transfer: European Review of Labour and Research*, 28(1): 83–100.

Milkman, R. (1976) 'Women's work and economic crisis', *Review of Radical Political Economics*, 8(1): 73–97.

Sallaz, J. (2919) 'Service labor and symbolic power: on putting Bourdieu to work', *Work and Occupations*, 37(3): 295–319.

Schmitter, P. (1974) 'Still the century of corporatism?', *The Review of Politics*, 36(1): 85–131.

Schmitter, P. and Grote, J. (1997) 'The corporatist Sisyphus: past, present and future', EUI SPS Working Paper 1997/04.

Schnabel, C. (2013) 'Union membership and density: some (not so) stylized facts and challenges', *European Journal of Industrial Relations*, 19(3): 255–72.

Silver, B. (2003) *Forces of Labour: Workers' Movements and Globalization since 1870*, Cambridge: Cambridge University Press.

Standing, G. (2011) *The Precariat: The New Dangerous Class*, London: Bloomsbury.

Streeck, W. (2016) *How Will Capitalism End? Essays on a Failing System*, London: Verso.

Thompson, P. (2010) 'The capitalist labour process: concepts and connections', *Capital and Class*, 34(1): 7–14.

Walton, R.E. and McKersie, R.B. (1965) A Behavioral Theory of Labor Negotiations: An Analysis of a Social Interaction System, Ithaca, NY: ILR Press.

Webb, S. and Webb, B. (1894) *The History of Trade Unionism*, London: Longmans, Green and Co.

Webb, S. and Webb, B. (1897) *Industrial Democracy,* London: Longmans, Green & Co.

4

Embedded Bedfellows: Industrial Relations and (Analytical) Human Resource Management

Tony Dundon and Adrian Wilkinson

Introduction

Human resource management (HRM), as a field of study, has evolved since its entry onto a 1980s' 'enterprise culture' that prized ideological individualism and hard business performance (Guest, 1990). In this chapter, we argue that HRM can have three uses: 'as a field of study', addressing factors influencing how people are managed; as a specific model delivering firm-level 'competitive advantage', for example, high-commitment management (HCM) or high-performance work systems (HPWS); or as a 'normative perspective', for example, searching for best practice or best-fit human resource (HR) arrangements. We suggest that approaching HRM 'as a field of study' reflects a more eclectic and pluralist approach concerned with external contextual forces, as well as internal social relationship dynamics (see Boxall and Purcell, 2016; Dundon et al, 2022).

Within the realm of work and employment, 'human resource management' threatened to supplant the nomenclature of 'industrial relations' (IR), which has rather different epistemological and ontological underpinnings (Ackers and Wilkinson, 2003). With the decline of institutional IR (Purcell, 1993), contemporary HRM was seen by some to fill gaps in the coverage of modern working life shaped by the emergent 'enterprise culture' of the 1980s. While there were some battles in the 1980s and into the early 1990s around the distinctions between personnel management (PM) and HRM (Guest, 1987), or whether HRM and IR had arrived at an accommodation of some common ground related to issues of work and employment, by the new millennium, there was an altogether different threat to both IR and HRM in terms of the intellectual space from a growing psychologization of the subject area (Godard, 2014; Kaufman, 2020; Barry and Wilkinson, 2021).

While being seen as part of a US neoliberal and hyper-individualistic agenda, HRM has evolved, at least in the UK, to reflect a variety of approaches, with each of which seeking to understand the tensions and issues affecting people in work and employment. We acknowledge that this HRM mix can be seen much more in the likes of the UK, Ireland, Australia and New Zealand than in North America, where HRM has been seen more as applied psychology and IR is often seen as a branch of labour economics (Kaufman, 2014). It is possible that HR as a broader field of study has something of a unique multidisciplinary antecedent that evolved out of earlier IR scholarship, including sociology, law, heterodox economics, political science, history and psychology. Indeed, approaches to studying the subject of HRM in the UK were first developed by former leading IR scholars: Keith Sisson, Director of the Industrial Relations Research Unit (IRRU) at Warwick University and founding editor of the *Human Resource Management Journal* (*HRMJ*); followed by John Storey and then John Purcell, a former president of British Universities Industrial Relations Association (BUIRA) (1995–98) and author of *Good Industrial Relations* (Purcell, 1981); and, finally, Mick Marchington as *HRMJ* editor, who was author of *Managing Industrial Relations* (Marchington, 1982). Around the same time, other new journals included: *The International Journal of Human Resource Management* (*IJHRM*), founded by Michael Poole, an industrial sociologist, who had published books on industrial democracy; and *Personnel Review* (*PR*), edited by Karen Legge, who wrote some of the most influential critiques of HRM (Legge, 1995). One of the earliest advocates of HRM in the UK was David Guest (1990), and while an organizational psychologist, he advanced a pluralist tradition within the subject area, was a former editor of the *British Journal of Industrial Relations* (*BJIR*) and was previously based at the Industrial Relations Department in the London School of Economics (LSE).

We ourselves have come from an IR background but teach and research work and employment issues under the rubric of HRM as a broad field of study. Here, we follow the path of 'analytical' HRM suggested by Boxall et al (2007: 5), in that we agree:

> the fundamental mission of the academic management discipline of HRM is not to propagate perceptions of 'best practice' in 'excellent companies' but, most of all, to identify and explain what happens in practice. Analytical HRM privileges explanation over prescription. The primary task of analytical HRM is to build theory and gather empirical data to account for the way management actually behaves in organizing work and managing people across different jobs, workplaces, companies, industries, and societies.

In presenting this short overview, the chapter first reviews the development of HRM as a subject. Then, we discuss ambiguity regarding its meaning, followed several different approaches as to how the subject has been studied. The issue of context and influence shaping HRM are then briefly outlined, before some future challenges to the subject are reviewed.

The development of HRM

If we appreciate HRM as a set of processes and activities associated with managing people in employment, then the subject has a long pedigree. According to Kaufman (2014), many of the core aspects of HRM could be found among many large US organizations in the early 1900s. Historically, the development of business paternalism and, in particular, industrial welfare placed greater emphasis on supporting labour, including the religious beliefs of Quakers, with housing and social amenities (for example, Cadbury's at Bourneville, Unilever on Merseyside or Guinness in Dublin and London) (see Strangleman, 2019).

Of course, how people were managed was not called 'human resource management' at the time. Evolving from the scientific management of F.W. Taylor (see Cullinane and Cushen, 2019) and the human relations studies of Elton Mayo (see Bruce and Nyland, 2017), there emerged a more concerted effort at administrative efficiency through job design, payment systems, time and motion, record keeping, and, later, experts drafted in to negotiate around the 'labour problem' (Cullinane, 2018). As union membership expanded, personnel management often included within it an IR function (or manager), which added a newer degree of managerial 'professionalism' to how people were managed at work (Gospel, 2019).

Notwithstanding oversimplification, the goals of administrative efficiency typically associated with personnel management around the 1950s–1980s (Torrington, 1998) led to a new (so-called) 'strategic orientation' in the name of HRM around post-1980 (Wilkinson, 2022). The claims of HRM to enhance corporate performance and engender greater workforce commitment caught the attention of business leaders and executives, initially in the US (Fombrun et al, 1984) and later the UK (Guest, 1987; Storey, 1992).

Among UK (and other) scholars, an eclectic social-science critique sought to unpack the meanings and implications of HRM as an approach rather than endorse its upbeat and performance-enhancing properties (see Blyton and Turnbull, 1992; Legge, 1995; Boxall and Purcell, 2016). The subject evolved differently across the Atlantic, with US HRM more interested in an organization-level model of HRM inspired by the stream of research on HPWS (see Strauss, 2001; Ackers and Wilkinson, 2003). This approach combines theories and concepts from strategic management and organizational behaviour with a focus on resources and processes internal to the organization, and tends to lean towards a unitarist/shareholder perspective. We can see this in the differences in the two HR journals, where in the US, unlike *HRMJ*, *Human Resource Management* (*HRM*) editors have tended to be from a more applied psychology or strategy background.

These differences in use and approach to HRM have both added clarity to its meaning and reinforced its ambiguity (Keenoy, 1999). 'Human resource management' may be used as a label instead of 'personnel management' or 'industrial relations' (Guest, 1987), while for others, there are unique qualities which signal that it is something different and more strategic when managing people at work (Storey, 1992; see also Harney et al, 2018). More recent additions add yet another nomenclature to the mix of definitional ambiguity, that of 'talent management', claimed to offer a differential HR architecture that provides greater reward for those people that management regard as occupying a 'pivotal' position (Collings et al, 2019). However, such an approach has been criticized as 'old wine' in yet another 'new bottle' by describing the same sets of activities associated with HRM under the label 'talent' (Collings, 2014). It has been argued that talent management can result in potentially discriminatory outcomes by privileging a selected core group of employees, typically those with customer-facing roles, in contrast to peripheral employees, or when managers (subjectively) view workers as marginal (Dundon and Rafferty, 2018). Moreover, these debates mean that there is wide scope in how HRM is defined and therefore how the subject is both researched and taught in mainstream business schools.

Defining HRM: a case of definitional ambiguity?

Definitions of what is precisely meant by HRM have differed over time and space, with no single uniform definition and with variations over HRM as an analytical field of study, as a prescriptive model to improve corporate performance or as a normative approach in search of so-called 'best practice'. Each of these create different points of tension with IR and other academic approaches, such as labour process or work sociology. As a field of study, HRM might be viewed as covering different terrain but including some overlapping areas with IR. In contrast, as a performance-driven model, it is seen as an alternative, and one that may undermine IR (or at least trade unions).

As well as the subject focus, there are concerns with regards to the normative leanings: 'what is good for the firm must be good for the worker' is predominantly unitarist in assuming that the company will, or should have, a single source of authority. Where it exists, conflict is irrational, unnecessary or a product of the wrong policy or misunderstandings among the workforce, and can be engineered out of an organization through more sophisticated HR policy. Problematically, such a view is ambivalent on collective bargaining and trade unionism, or, at best, regards them as unnecessary (Harney et al, 2018). The strong flavour of unitarism, especially from US and industrial and organizational (I&O) psychology variants of HRM, can be illustrated in its discussion of employee involvement and participation. For example, management encourage worker voice to emerge only on their terms; for some scholars, 'to vent or complain' is not seen as employee voice (Morrison, 2011: 375). Such a perspective does not envisage employee voice as being based on interests other than those of the employer (Barry and Wilkinson, 2016). In contrast, IR incorporates facets of labour indeterminacy, antagonism, reward–effort exchange, conflict 'and' cooperation, as well as multiple voice channels. For much of the global labour force, like those crammed into factory dormitories in China making our smartphones, the casual workforce comprising the agri-food sector or those delivering food and other packages via the gig economy during the COVID-19 pandemic, the latest HR fads of 'engagement', 'agility' or 'talent' seem not only irrelevant but also ignorant of structural inequalities and employer power (Dundon et al, 2017).

However, the approaches to HRM are not either a pure undiluted strain of hyper-individualism and unitarism from the US or an orthodox IR tradition concerned with the institutions of job regulation and collective bargaining. There is considerable nuance and variation in between, including hybrid approaches that study the employment relationship by drawing on multidisciplinary schools of thought, or what might be a more blended worker-centric human resource and employment relations (HRER) leaning, as developed by some of the earlier UK scholars.

We therefore suggest an 'inclusive' definition of HRM centred on recognizing multiple internal employment relationship dynamics, alongside wider external economic, regulatory and socio-political forces shaping employer choices and workforce conditions. We thus define HRM as 'the formation and enactment of policies designed to manage the employment of people in an organisation' (Dundon and Wilkinson, 2021: 4), to which there can be a range of competing approaches or schools of thought.

Competing approaches to the study of HRM

There is, of course, debate between definitional terms, for example between 'human resources', 'personnel', 'industrial' or 'employment relations', 'organizational psychology', or the baggage associated with recent fad of 'talent management'. Either way, the label may be less important than the ontological and epistemological underpinnings of what is being studied (Ackers and Wilkinson, 2003; Edwards, 2006; Dundon et al, 2017). Unitarist overtones may not only signal managerial bias but also lead to a cul-de-sac given the assumption that everyone is (supposedly) working towards the same unitary (corporate) goal (Cullinane and Dundon, 2014). That is to say, workers and managers, employers and shareholders, and unions can all have competing objectives as well as seek company success (Cullinane, 2018). These sorts of debates give rise to a range of social-science approaches to the study of HRM, as summarized in Table 4.1.

Table 4.1 captures several different approaches to the study of HRM. It seeks to reflect a diversity of approaches involving: (1) industrial relations, labour process and critical management scholars who teach and research on HRM issues and topics (see Ackers and Wilkinson, 2003); and (2) the more managerialist variants (see Fombrun et al, 1984; Wright and Snell, 1998; Wright et al, 2011). The first set of approaches are drawn from the managerial-driven tradition, described as 'matching HR schools of thought'. The 'hard' style of HRM (Fombrun et al, 1984) tends to see employees as a resource to be used to secure efficiency. In this approach, employees are no more valuable than capital equipment or land assets. The rationale is business-driven efficiency, and management are highly unitarist in seeking to deliver organizational goals. In contrast is a 'softer' variant of the matching school (Beer et al, 1984), which seeks wider stakeholder inclusion and takes a social systems perspective.

'Organizational performance' can be considered another approach to the study of HRM, closely aligned with the unitarist and US version of HRM of the matching models. It claims universal appeal in terms of presenting a set of complementary HR activities that can add to corporate performance, often via enhancements to employee effort and commitment (see, among others, Pfeffer, 1998; Bowen and Ostroff, 2004). Many of these studies seek to quantify statistically the links between a bundle of HR policies and performance outcomes (Huselid, 1995), though it has been argued that performance measures can equate to increased work pressure for employees (Ramsay et al, 2000).

A third school may be described as an 'employee-centric approach'. It is more reflective of how people are managed from a broader pluralist approach regarding how scholars interpret individual concerns along with external contextual influences and collective structures for employee involvement and consultation (Sisson, 1994; Bacon, 2003; Boxall and Purcell, 2016; Marchington et al, 2020; Dobbins et al, 2021). The role of line managers as potential change agents in shaping employee experiences of work is important in the processes that may balance competing interests for efficiency, equity and voice (Budd, 2004).

In more recent years, the disciplines of organizational behaviour (OB) and I&O psychology have led to claims about a growing 'psychologization of HRM' as a potentially distinct approach (Dundon and Wilkinson, 2021). On the one hand, the academic discipline of psychology has had a robust

Table 4.1: Different schools of thought on the study of HRM

School of thought	Definitional assumption	Orientation	(Anticipated) role of managers	(Expected) role of workers
Matching model (hard)	Performance compliance Unitarist	Efficiency driven Short-term returns	Rule-bound	Compliant Disposable
Matching model (soft)	Efficiency Well-being Pluralist (and unitarist)	Supporting stakeholders Longer-term consequences	Coaching styles	Empowered
Organizational performance	High performance objectives Unitarist	HR policy fit (internal and external) with outcomes	Key performance indicator (KPI) driven	Discretionary (intensified) work effort
Employee-centric approach	Critical of performance assumptions Pluralist (and unitarist)	Goals to balance competing and supporting interests	Change agents	Individual and collective alliances
Psychologization of HRM	Support corporate (managerial) actions Unitarist	Internal I&O psychology to leverage change	Behavioural control (from above)	Individual behavioural incentives
Radical (critical) perspective	Extracting surplus value from labour Radical pluralist	Power/globalization Neoliberalism Financialization	Manipulative control Agents of owners	Compliance and resistance of control

Source: Adapted from Dundon and Wilkinson (2021: 6)

place in industrial relations and HR-related work (Hertzberg et al, 1959; Troth and Guest, 2019). However, on the other hand, a series of articles have raised concerns around a growing micro-focus and unitary approach to HRM (Godard, 2014; Budd, 2020; Kaufman, 2020). These concerns are about the approach of I&O psychology, with a reliance on so-called 'scientific' (quantitative and positivist) methods to the neglect of other social-science insights (such as industrial relations, sociology, critical management studies and so on), and its focus on micro and individual traits to the neglect of collective systems for people management (such as trade unions, works councils and so on). Kaufman (2020: 64) argues the concern is not psychology per se as a legitimate school of thought but its 'ization' into the HRM space by reducing explanations of macro level forces to individual worker difference and psychological behaviours.

Finally, the critical management studies and labour process traditions have contributed to debates on HRM, albeit spanning different epistemological boundaries. Notably, some of the most-cited contributions on HRM have been advanced by scholars from a critical and/or radically informed perspective (such as Legge, 1995; Keenoy, 1999; Thompson, 2011). While there is always a danger of conflating different variants under a single label, in outline, the more critical schools articulate a healthy scepticism regarding management actions and motives. There is typically a broader objective to advance knowledge and understanding regarding the various tensions, ambiguities and dynamics affecting how people are controlled, yet also how employers seek to engender commitment at work, often with an eye on external macro and meso forces of capitalism and their impacts on social relationships and wider (in)equalities from employment.

As suggested, presenting so-called different schools of thought can oversimplify matters with considerable overlap. Therefore, we note, for example, that psychological contributions have inspired debate about the quality of working life and job redesign from a more critical and pluralist interpretation (Holman, 2013). The Tavistock Institute of Human Relations (TIHR) has advanced collective and individual policy insights, while sociology, economics, post-structural analysis and political discourses have all shaped the field of work, employment and HRM.

Contexts matter

Even the more 'upbeat' and highly 'managerialist' approaches to HRM, from the likes of Pfeffer (1998) or Ulrich et al (2007), acknowledge that contextual factors matter to our understanding of how people are managed in work (Cooke, 2018). Furthermore, how rules and policies are enacted and regulated remain important factors in our understanding, notably, the source of power of the nation state (Martínez Lucio and MacKenzie, 2018;

Wilkinson and Barry, 2020). Following external crisis and global pandemics, organizations have restructured, reduced their workforces, made cuts and decentralized operations. At the same time, many corporations have profited and expanded during the pandemic. For example, Amazon increased its revenue by almost one third during COVID-19 restrictions from home and online sales. Yet, it has been criticized for failing to protect workers' health and safety during the pandemic while also aggressively resisting workers joining a union (see Day and Eidelson, 2021; *The Guardian*, 2021).

A problem with much of the prescriptive HR literature is that in such accounts, as the short Amazon illustration depicts, external economic shocks and factors are seen to be outside of management's control. This may be true for many managers. However, there are arguments that employers utilize shocks and crisis to push through change and workforce restructuring they may otherwise not pursue (Crouch, 2013). For example, large multinational corporations (MNCs) have been shown to affect the HR arrangements and conditions within smaller firms in their supply-chain network (Almond and Gonzalez Menendez, 2014; Reinecke et al, 2018; Chan et al, 2020).

The global COVID-19 pandemic has led to untold harm. Unlike the Global Financial Crisis of 2008, the pandemic is both a public health and economic crisis. As a unique and unprecedented circumstance, it has placed organizations and HR managers into new uncharted waters in terms of how to respond, with a whole raft of HRM and people-management implications that are not yet fully realized or understood (Collings et al, 2021). While there have been different responses globally from various governments and organizations, the importance of labour market institutions regulating work and employment standards during a crisis appears crucial (Dobbins et al, 2023). However, it would be rare to find a chapter in an HRM textbook that considers the role of the state per se (see Martínez Lucio, 2022).

Various context factors matter, even when there is no immediate or obvious global shock. The economy, market turbulence, technology, changes to social values and attitudes, laws, and the power resources of different institutions are, for the most part, slow to effect change. Indeed, as Eccles et al (1992) historical review of change shows, managers typically view and describe their organizational environment as turbulent and continuously in a state of transformation. The implications for HRM will vary across companies. Some sectors and industries have seen an increasing feminization of work, where increasing numbers of women enter occupations (many lower paid and lower skilled), with reported gender pay gaps and inequalities across society (Muzio and Tomlinson, 2012; Rubery et al, 2016). The use of 'non-standard employment relationships' (NSER) has grown considerably, leaving many subject to insecure work, zero-hours contracts and casual/temporary forms of employment, with an HR approach that might be about cost cutting as much as its earlier welfare traditions.

The future of HRM as a field of study

The way HRM is taught and researched may be shaped by disciplinary boundaries and competing perspectives as to how the management of work and employees is framed (Heery, 2016). For some, the precise nomenclature of 'human resource management', 'personnel management' or 'industrial relations' indicates important distinctions that have very different ideological and ontological antecedents. For others, the labels are less important than what is being analysed and how employment conditions are decided and acted upon. We are probably closer to the latter as a broad eclectic and pluralist field of study concerned with the processes and factors affecting working conditions, employment rights and organizational and managerial decision making (Dobbins et al, 2021; Dundon et al, 2022).

On the one hand, as a profession, HRM appears hearty. In the UK, the number of enterprises with a senior HR manager in situ has increased (van Wanrooy et al, 2013). Some suggest that the COVID-19 pandemic has allowed HR to come of age, with examples of what might be termed the 'pluralist HR professional', allowing some employees a new degree of control and empowerment over their own work arrangements, such as choosing home or remote working (see Kulik, 2022). In addition, the growth of university departments and degree programmes, many with professional accreditation, have also increased in the HR space. As a practitioner body, the Chartered Institute of Personnel and Development (CIPD) has over 160,000 members and commissions research conducted by academics (and others), with access to government and other policy stakeholders to potentially influence employment regulations. In terms of research 'impact', as defined by the likes of Research Excellence Framework (REF) metrics in the UK, HRM and employment relations have produced some of the higher-quality impact case reports, with widespread influence and activist engagement among multiple stakeholders outside of academia (Thomas and Turnbull, 2021).

Future HR challenges include concerns about the capabilities of the profession to respond to big-ticket transformations in the world of work, such as new technologies, the climate crisis and demographic change (Hughes and Dundon, 2023). Arguably, advances in new technologies have considerable potential to improve working lives and employment conditions rather than be preoccupied with corporate profit per se. The International Labour Organization (ILO, 2019), for instance, has a policy agenda for 'decent work' standards globally, which includes, among other aspects, better use and more equitable integration of technologies to sustain jobs in the future (Berg et al, 2018). Grimshaw and Rani (2021) review the challenges for HR in terms of managing work transitions from dirty polluting industries to a greener and environmentally sustainable future. The role of the state will be key. Problematically, with minimalist government intervention and the contextual forces of neoliberalism in many countries, HR managers may continue in a 'business-as-usual' mindset, with little proactive change (Grimshaw and Rani, 2021). There are opportunities for HR to support workers in terms of reskilling out of polluting sectors (for example, coal) and champion a business-case rationale for more environmentally friendly jobs, including support for those employees with care responsibilities, without any loss to pay or career prospects. At the same time, however, power relations matter, and it is equally feasible that despite good intentions from the more pluralist of HR managers to try and make things better, imbalances of power mean that such contestation is part and parcel of an analytically informed approach to the study of HRM.

Conclusion

This chapter has offered a short review of HRM and its relationship to IR. It has considered its evolution, definitional ambiguity and associated debates. It has presented HRM as a broad subject that has evolved from earlier social-science disciplines concerned with work and the 'labour problem', including law, sociology, economics, IR, history and psychology. We suggest that as a field of study, asking how people are managed at work and why they encounter certain employment experiences helps move beyond the prescriptive 'how to do' flavour associated with other managerialist interpretations of HRM. Perhaps the older debates between PM and HRM, or HR and IR, have moved on, and the more pressing threats these days include a creeping managerialism and a shifting centre of gravity towards unitarism (which are colonizing the spaces for pluralist and critical areas of inquiry in the university business school). As a broad church concerned about the management of employment, HRM can inspire future students when taught through a critical lens, drawing on a rich and multidisciplinary research paradigm that has an established track record of influencing wider policy debates and practices.

References
Ackers, P. and Wilkinson, A. (2003) 'The British industrial relations tradition: formation, breakdown and salvage', in P. Ackers and A. Wilkinson (eds) *Understanding Work & Employment: Industrial Relations in Transition*, Oxford: Oxford University Press, pp 1–27.
Almond, P. and Gonzalez Menendez, M.C. (2014) 'The changing nature of HRM, organisational change and globalization', in M. Martínez Lucio (ed) *International Human Resource Management: An Employment Relations Perspective*, London: Sage, pp 37–56.
Bacon, N. (2003) 'HRM and industrial relations', in P. Ackers and A. Wilkinson (eds) *Understanding Work and Employment: Industrial Relations in Transition*, Oxford: Oxford University Press, pp 71–88.

Barry, M. and Wilkinson, A. (2016) 'Pro-social or pro-management? A critique of the conception of employee voice as a pro-social behaviour within organizational behaviour', *British Journal of Industrial Relations*, 54(2): 261–84.

Barry, M. and Wilkinson, A. (2021) 'Employee voice, psychologisation and human resource management (HRM)', *Human Resource Management Journal*, 32(3): 631–46.

Beer, M., Spector, B., Lawrence, P., Quinn, Mills, D. and Walton, R. (1984) *Managing Human Assets*, London: Collier Macmillan.

Berg, J., Furrer, M., Harmon, E., Rani, U. and Silberman, M. (2018) *Digital Labour Platforms and the Future of Work: Towards Decent Work in the Online World*, ILO: Geneva.

Blyton, P. and Turnbull, P. (eds) (1992) *Reassessing Human Resource Management*, London: Sage.

Bowen, D. and Ostroff, C. (2004) 'Understanding HRM–performance linkages: the role of the "strength" of the HRM system', *Academy of Management Review*, 29(2): 202–22.

Boxall, P. and Purcell, J. (2016) *Strategy and Human Resource Management*, 4th edn, New York: Palgrave Macmillan.

Boxall, P., Purcell, J. and Wright, P. (2007) 'Human resource management: scope, analysis, and significance', in P. Boxall, J. Purcell and P. Wright (eds) *The Oxford Handbook of Human Resource Management*, Oxford: Oxford University Press, pp 1–16.

Bruce, K. and Nyland, C. (2017) 'Human relations', in A Wilkinson, S. Armstrong and M. Lounsbury (eds) *The Oxford Handbook of Management*, Oxford: OUP, pp 39–56.

Budd, J. (2004) *Employment with a Human Face: Balancing Efficiency, Equity and Voice*, Ithaca, NY: ILR Press.

Budd, J. (2020) 'The psychologisation of employment relations, alternative models of the employment relationship, and the OB turn', *Human Resource Management Journal*, 30(1): 73–83.

Chan, J., Selden, M. and Pun, N. (2020) *Dying for an iPhone: Apple, Foxconn, and the Lives of China's Workers*, Chicago, IL: Haymarket Books.

Collings, D.G. (2014) 'Toward mature talent management: beyond shareholder value', *Human Resource Development Quarterly*, 25(3): 301–19.

Collings, D.G., Mellahi, K. and Cascio, W.F. (2019) 'Global talent management and performance in multinational enterprises: a multilevel perspective', *Journal of Management*, 45(2): 540–66.

Collings, D.G., Nyberg, A.J., Wright, P.M. and McMackin, J. (2021) 'Leading through paradox in a COVID-19 world: human resources comes of age', *Human Resource Management Journal*, 31(4): 819–33.

Cooke, F.L. (2018) 'Concepts, contexts, and mindsets: putting human resource management research in perspectives', *Human Resource Management Journal*, 28(1): 1–13.

Crouch, C. (2013) *Making Capitalism Fit for Society*, London: Polity.

Cullinane, N. (2018) 'The field of employment relations: a review', in A. Wilkinson, T. Dundon, J. Donaghey and A. Colvin (eds) *The Routledge Companion to Employment Relations*, London: Routledge, pp 23–36.

Cullinane, N. and Cushen, J. (2019) 'Applying scientific management to modern employment relations and HRM', in K. Townsend, K. Cafferkey, A. McDermott and T. Dundon (eds) *Elgar Introduction to Theories of Human Resources and Employment Relations*, Cheltenham: Edward Elgar, pp 53–66.

Cullinane, N. and Dundon, T. (2014) 'Unitarism and employer resistance to trade unionism', *International Journal of Human Resource Management*, 25(18): 2573– 90.

Day, M. and Eidelson, J. (2021) 'For Amazon workers, winning union vote would be just a first step', *Bloomberg Businessweek*, 10 March. Available at: www.bloomberg.com/news/articles/2021-03-10/amazon-amzn-union-fight-will-continue-even-if-alabama-workers-vote-to-unionize

Dobbins, T., Hughes, E. and Dundon, T. (2021) '"Zones of contention" in industrial relations: framing pluralism as praxis', *Journal of Industrial Relations*, 63(2): 149–76.

Dobbins, T., Johnstone, S., Kahancova, M., Lamare, J.R. and Wilkinson, A. (2023) 'Comparative impacts of the COVID-19 pandemic on work and employment – why industrial relations institutions matter', *Industrial Relations: A Journal of Economy & Society*, 62(2): 115–25.

Dundon, T. and Rafferty, A. (2018) 'The (potential) demise of HRM?', *Human Resource Management Journal*, 28(3): 377–91.

Dundon, T. and Wilkinson, A. (2021) 'Human resource management: a contemporary perspective', in A. Wilkinson, T. Dundon and T. Redman (eds) *Contemporary HRM: Texts and Cases*, London: Sage, pp 3–30.

Dundon, T., Cullinane, N. and Wilkinson, A. (2017) *A Very Short, Fairly Interesting and Reasonably Cheap Book about Employment Relations*, London: Sage.

Dundon, T., Wilkinson, A. and Ackers, P. (2022) 'Mapping employee involvement and participation in institutional context: Mick Marchington's applied pluralist contributions to human resource management research methods, theory and policy', *Human Resource Management Journal*, 33(3): 551–63.

Eccles, R.G., Nohria, N. and Berkley, J.D. (1992) *Beyond the Hype: Rediscovering the Essence of Management*, Boston, MA: Harvard Business School Press.

Edwards, P.K. (2006) 'Industrial relations and critical realism: IR's tacit contribution', Warwick Papers in Industrial Relations 80, March.

Fombrun, C.J., Tichy, N.M. and Devanna, M.A. (1984) *Strategic Human Resource Management*, New York: Wiley.

Godard, J. (2014) 'The psychologisation of employment relations?', *Human Resource Management Journal*, 24(1): 1–18

Gospel, H. (2019) 'Human resource management: a historical perspective', in A. Wilkinson, N. Bacon, T. Redman and S. Snell (eds) *The SAGE Handbook of Human Resource Management*, London: SAGE, pp 12–29.

Grimshaw, D. and Rani, U. (2021) 'The future of work: facing the challenges of new technologies, climate change and ageing', in A. Wilkinson, T. Dundon and T. Redman (eds) *Contemporary Human Resource Management: Text and Cases*, 6th edn, London: Sage, pp 557–87.

The Guardian (2021) 'New York sues Amazon over claims it failed to protect workers from pandemic', 17 February. Available at: www.theguardian.com/technology/2021/feb/17/amazon-sued-new-york-failure-protect-workers-pandemic-claims

Guest, D.E. (1987) 'Human resource management and industrial relations', *Journal of Management Studies*, 24: 503–21.

Guest, D.E. (1990) 'Human resource management and the American dream', *Journal of Management Studies*, 27: 377–97.

Harney, B., Dundon, T. and Wilkinson, A. (2018) 'Employment relations and human resource management', in A. Wilkinson, T. Dundon, J. Donaghey and A. Colvin (eds) *The Routledge Companion to Employment Relations*, Abingdon: Routledge, pp 122–38.

Heery, E. (2016) *Framing Work: Unitary, Pluralist, and Critical Perspectives in the Twenty-First Century*, London: Oxford University Press.

Herzberg, F., Mausner, B. and Snyderman, B. (1959) *The Motivation to Work*, New York: Wiley.

Holman, D. (2013) 'Job types and job quality in Europe', *Human Relations*, 66(4): 475–502.

Hughes, E. and Dundon, T. (2023) 'Addressing big societal challenges in HRM research: a society–actors–processes–policy framework', *Academy of Management Perspectives*, 37(2): 91–116.

Huselid, M. (1995) 'The impact of human resource management practices on turnover, productivity and corporate financial performance', *Academy of Management Journal*, 38(3): 635–72.

ILO (International Labour Organization) (2019) *Global Commission on the Future of Work*, Geneva: ILO.

Kaufman, B. (2014) *Development of HRM across Nations: Unity and Diversity*, Cheltenham: Edward Elgar.

Kaufman, B. (2020) 'The real problem: the deadly combination of psychologisation, scientism, and normative promotionalism takes strategic human resource management down a 30-year dead end', *Human Resource Management Journal*, 30(4): 49–72.

Keenoy, T. (1999) 'HRM as hologram: a polemic', *Journal of Management Studies*, 36: 1–23.

Kulik, C.T. (2022) 'We need a hero: HR and the "next normal" workplace', *Human Resource Management Journal*, 32(1): 216–31.

Legge, K. (1995) *Human Resource Management: Rhetorics and Realities*, London: Macmillan.

Marchington, M. (1982) *Managing Industrial Relations*, London: McGraw Hill.

Marchington, M., Kynighou, A., Donnelly, R. and Wilkinson, A. (2020) *Human Resource Management at Work*, London: CIPD Publishing.

Martínez Lucio, M. (2022) 'Continuities and change in national employment relations: the role of politics and ideas', in M. Martínez Lucio and R. MacKenzie (eds) *International Human Resource Management*, 2nd edn, London: Sage, pp 59–78.

Martínez Lucio, M. and MacKenzie, R. (2018) 'The state and employment relations: continuity and change in the politics of regulation', in A. Wilkinson, T. Dundon, J. Donaghey and A. Colvin (eds) *The Routledge Companion to Employment Relations*, London: Routledge, pp 157–74.

Morrison, E.W. (2011) 'Employee voice behaviour: integration and directions for future research', *Academy of Management Annals*, 5: 373–412.

Muzio, D. and Tomlinson, J. (2012) 'Gender, diversity and inclusion in professions and professional organizations: setting the scene and the agenda for research', *Gender, Work and Organization*, 19(5): 455–66.

Pfeffer, J. (1998) *The Human Equation*, New York: New York University Press.

Purcell, J. (1981) *Good Industrial Relations*, London: Palgrave Macmillan.

Purcell, J. (1993) 'The challenge of human resource management for industrial relations research and practice', *International Journal of Human Resource Management*, 4(3): 511–27.

Ramsay, H., Scholarios, D. and Harley, B. (2000) 'Employees and high-performance work systems: testing inside the black box', *British Journal of Industrial Relations*, 38(4): 501–31.

Reinecke, J., Donaghey, J., Wilkinson, A. and Wood, G. (2018) 'Global supply chains and social relations at work: brokering across boundaries', *Human Relations*, 71(4): 459–80.

Rubery, J., Keizer, A. and Grimshaw, D. (2016) 'Flexibility bites back: the multiple and hidden costs of flexible employment policies', *Human Resource Management Journal*, 26: 235–51.

Sisson, K. (ed) (1994) *Personnel Management (Second Edition)*, Oxford: Blackwell.

Storey, J. (1992) *Developments in the Management of Human Resources: An Analytical Review*, Oxford: Blackwell.

Strangleman, T. (2019) *Voices of Guinness: An Oral History of the Park Royal Brewery*, Oxford: OUP.

Strauss, G. (2001) 'HRM in the USA: correcting some British impressions', *International Journal of Human Resource Management*, 12(6): 873–97.

Thomas, H. and Turnbull, P. (2021) 'Activist research: excellence, impact & engagement in neo-liberal business schools', 16 February, Centre for Global Business (CGB), Monash University. Available at: www.youtube.com/watch?v=CLxKMaVHn3s

Thompson, P. (2011) 'The trouble with HRM', *Human Resource Management Journal*, 21(4): 355–67.

Torrington, D. (1998) 'Crisis and opportunity in HRM: the challenge for the personnel function', in P. Sparrow and M. Marchington (eds) *Human Resource Management: The New Agenda*, London: FT/Pitman, pp 23–36.

Troth, A.C. and Guest, D. E. (2019) 'The case for psychology in human resource management research', *Human Resource Management Journal*, 30(1): 34–48.

Ulrich, D., Brockbank, W., Johnson, D. and Younger, J. (2007) 'Human resource competencies: responding to increased expectations', *Employment Relations Today*, 34(3): 1–12.

Van Wanrooy, B., Bewley, H., Bryson, A., Forth, J., Freeth, S., Stokes, L. and Wood, S. (2013) *Employment Relations in the Shadow of Recession*, London: Palgrave Macmillan.

Wilkinson, A. (2022) *Human Resource Management: A Very Short Introduction*, Oxford: OUP.

Wilkinson, A. and Barry, M. (eds) (2020) *The Future of Work and Employment*, Cheltenham: Edward Elgar.

Wright, P. and Snell, S. (1998) 'Toward a unifying framework for exploring fit and flexibility in strategic human resource management', *Academy of Management Review*, 23(4): 756–72.

Wright, P., Boudreau, J., Pace, D., Sartain, L., McKinnon, P. and Antoine, R. (2011) *The Chief HR Officer: Defining the New Role of Human Resource Leaders*, San Francisco, CA: Jossey-Bass.

5

Trade Unions in a Changing World of Work

Melanie Simms

Introduction

Some 40 years ago, the term 'industrial relations' was often, wrongly, conflated with trade unionism. Unions were so embedded in the collective systems and institutions that regulate the employment relationship that it was challenging to imagine a setting where unions were not a dominant actor. Today, the role and influence of unions is much reduced, especially outside the public sector. Union membership, density and bargaining coverage in the UK have all declined dramatically since the 1980s, and with that, their role in public life and influence over employment terms and conditions has waned. This chapter reflects on these changes, how unions have attempted to reverse the decline and their role in contemporary society. Central to the analysis presented is the argument that unions both shape the broader economic and social context, and are shaped by them. Capitalism and labour markets have changed partly because unions have lost influence. Equally important is that the challenges unions face have changed because the wider social and economic contexts have changed. This dynamic interplay means that the future of work and of unions is very difficult to predict.

The decline of union influence does not mean that unions have no role in the contemporary regulation of work. Unions represent 6.4 million workers in the UK (around 23 per cent of working people) (BEIS, 2022). Unions regulate terms and conditions of work through multiple mechanisms: bargaining collectively; lobbying for changes to policies and laws; supporting members when they have problems at work; and working to enforce agreements in workplaces. Collective bargaining is a crucial role and allows unions to negotiate the terms and conditions for large groups of workers rather than individuals, whether or not they are individually members of that union. Estimates vary as to how many workers have their terms and conditions set by collective bargaining. The Labour Force Survey suggests that it is around 29 per cent, but the Annual Survey of Hours and Earnings (ASHE) estimates it at around 39 per cent (for an extensive discussion, see Waddington, 2019). Those headline figures hide significant differences between the public and private sectors. In the public sector, around 90 per cent of workers have collectively bargained terms and conditions, but this is only about 21 per cent of private sector workers (Waddington, 2019). Unions (both individually and through the umbrella Trades Union Congress [TUC]) have demonstrated their wider influence by shaping government responses and policies during the COVID-19 pandemic from 2020 onwards. At the same time, much more is known now about 'what works' to recruit and organize workers, both in workplaces where there is already the right to representation but where membership is low and in workplaces where there has not previously been a union presence. Therefore, although unions still very much have a place in the regulation of work and employment, this chapter argues that social and economic changes mean the challenges to union revitalization continue to limit opportunity for wider renewal.

In order to explore whether there would be opportunities for changing the wider context of the regulation of work and employment, the chapter first examines the reasons for the decline in union representation in the 1980s and 1990s, before reflecting on the legacy of the New Labour period of 1997–2010. The chapter argues that this extensive period of Labour Party governments shaped a new context for employment regulation in the UK but did not fundamentally change the fortunes of union membership and influence because of broader developments. The phenomenon known as 'financialization' increasingly shapes how organizations make decisions, including about staff. The resultant changes to labour markets, regulation and employment have created huge anxiety about the future of work, with little confidence that those futures will be shaped by anything other than the demands of capital. The COVID-19 crisis has exacerbated those anxieties but created some space in social policy, especially in the devolved jurisdictions of Wales, Northern Ireland and Scotland, to ask fundamental questions about the role of unions and the worker voice in the institutions of social and economic policy making.

Decline of union influence in the 1980s

In the UK, in common with many countries of Western Europe, the period from 1945 to the 1970s was marked by economic growth and prosperity based on a broadly shared view of Keynesian economic policies

(Schott, 1982). Collective bargaining was central to economic and social policy making, with extensive structures to agree the terms and conditions of work at industry and organizational levels (Brown, 1986), particularly in the manufacturing sector, which dominated the labour market. By the early 1970s, the oil crises and subsequent economic shocks led to profound concerns among politicians and policy makers about the effects of industrial relations structures, particularly the ability of strong local union representatives in such key sectors as the automotive industry to secure high wage settlements in a context of high inflation (Brown, 1986).

After a period of attempted reforms (for an overview of limited efforts at industrial relations reform, see Brown, 1986) and growing industrial action, Margaret Thatcher was elected as prime minister on a platform that put industrial relations at the centre of her Conservative Party manifesto. In the subsequent period of Conservative Party governments from 1979 to 1997, the landscape of UK industrial relations changed beyond recognition (Addison and Siebert, 2003). A series of statutory constraints on both how unions organized themselves and the feasibility and effectiveness of strike action had the cumulative effect of limiting the ability of unions to use strikes to pursue collective-bargaining objectives. State support for employers in the newspaper industry during key strikes reinforced the commitment of the Conservative Party to the underpinning principle of 'managerial prerogative' (the right of managers to manage as they saw fit). Withdrawal of support from highly unionized strategic industries, such as coal mining, further cemented a reshaping of the economic landscape and labour market.

The UK labour market gradually restructured towards a strong service base to the extent that hospitality and retail alone account for between 20 and 25 per cent of the UK labour force in 2023 (ONS, 2023). Those changes brought profound challenges to unions' ability to effectively organize and represent workers. Many service jobs are located in smaller (by workforce) workplaces than, for example, factories. Complex shift patterns mean that workers are coming and going at many times of the day, as well as sometimes night. Many workers are employed part-time and flex their hours on a daily or weekly basis, meaning that it is hard to be sure when people are working and when they are not. All of these things make it difficult for unions to organize in order to speak to workers, find out their concerns and recruit them to the union (Heery and Simms, 2008). Added challenges emerge from the fact that much of the service sector has high labour turnover and is staffed by relatively young workers, many of whom have other roles (students, carers, other jobs and so on) (Simms et al, 2018).

Unsurprisingly, these structural changes bring challenges for unions (Bryson and Gomez, 2005). Organizing and representing workers takes time and investment, often in the form of many conversations with people to understand the complexities of their work and the grievances they hold, before planning how to represent those views collectively. In no small part as a result of the structural changes of the workforce and the investment required to organize in new workplaces, UK union membership composition has lagged behind the wider changes of the labour market. UK union members are more likely to be older and have longer tenure in their current jobs than the wider workforce (BEIS, 2022). Young workers are also less likely to be union members because they tend to be employed in occupations where there are fewer opportunities to join a union (Cha et al, 2019). As a result, unions have invested heavily in organizing to reach new groups, though with varying degrees of success (Simms et al, 2018).

One of the most profound consequences of these developments is that collective bargaining became less effective as a mechanism for determining the terms and conditions of work (Machin, 1997), even where it proved resilient. This has been particularly evident in low-wage sectors like retail and hospitality for a long time, and the election of the New Labour governments in the period from 1997 to 2010 marked a notable change in policies towards trade unions and labour market regulation more generally.

The New Labour era: efforts at institutional reform

In the 1990s, the Labour Party was deeply concerned about the potential political consequences of being seen as too similar to the party it was in the 1970s, especially with regard to its relationship with trade unions. Three policy directions relevant to the issues under discussion here emerged as a result: (1) establishing a floor of statutory minimum employment rights; (2) experimenting with forms of social partnership (as it was called then; now, it is more usually referred to as 'social dialogue') between employer and worker representative organizations (the Confederation of British Industry and TUC, respectively); and (3) providing mechanisms for unions to try to rebuild their workplace presence (for more detailed discussion, see Smith and Morton, 2006). Each is important in explaining the current context facing unions and so is considered in more detail.

As union influence declined and managerial prerogative was increasingly asserted during the 1980s, the limitations of regulating employment through collective agreements became clear. Policy makers and politicians, especially on the Left, became increasingly concerned about downward pressure on wages and the associated social problems of a low-wage economy (McIlroy, 1998). Focus turned to providing a floor of minimum rights and, in particular, the National Minimum Wage (NMW). The Labour Party's commitment to implementing European Union (EU) directives relating to the labour market – thereby overturning the negotiated opt-out for the UK – also ensured that a raft of employment rights deriving from the EU were transposed into UK law relatively quickly after the 1997 general election.

Together, these provided a new landscape of individual employment rights that acted to 'fill in' across what had become a largely deregulated private sector (Dickens and Hall, 2003).

In introducing both the NMW and some of the EU directives, the Labour governments introduced new forms of what is now called 'social dialogue' but at the time was called 'social partnership'. A range of forums allowed employer representatives and unions to negotiate the details and practicalities of specific areas of employment regulation. Ranging from such bodies as the Low Pay Commission (LPC), which has statutory underpinnings, to more informal but clearly instituted processes to agree the transposition of, for example, working-time regulations, there was a renewed commitment to bipartite and tripartite decision making, which gave unions a voice to represent not just members but workers more broadly. This involvement of unions was an important shift of policy making approach and strongly reinforced the idea that unions are the legitimate representatives of workers.

A third strand of activity was also very important during this period: the laws enacted to help unions gain recognition for collective bargaining where employers were resistant. The UK has a strong history of voluntarism in industrial relations, which, among other things, privileges the idea that employers should not be compelled to bargain collectively if they do not wish to. Therefore, the introduction of a procedure that could compel a reluctant employer to deal with a union was a notable change of regulatory direction. While being an indication of the support for union bargaining within workplaces, the hurdles to impose recognition were high and the government argued that it was very much up to unions to demonstrate that it was the will of the workers within the bargaining unit to move to collective negotiations. On balance, it is probably fair to summarize the long-term effects of this legislation as being an important signal of intent but having relatively minor effects on the numbers of workers covered by collective bargaining (Cumbers, 2005).

Union renewal efforts: 1990s and beyond

While it would be wrong to suggest that the landscape of employment regulation changed overnight on 1 May 1997, there was a notable renewed confidence in the trade union movement from the election of the first New Labour government. By 1999, the TUC had launched a training programme to develop a cadre of paid union officers specializing in organizing in both workplaces that already had recognition for collective bargaining and new workplaces. Drawing heavily on similar initiatives in the US and Australia, and learning from their experience in these areas, as well as labour history, the TUC Organising Academy was the flagship programme in a suite of initiatives intended to take advantage of this changed landscape (Simms et al, 2013).

During the subsequent years, the UK trade union movement learned a great deal about what works – and what does not – when organizing workers. 'Organizing' is a term that brings together a set of ideas that unions should encourage workers, and especially members, to take responsibility for working collectively to pursue their interests rather than relying on the professional expertise of union officers. Of course, professional union officers are often needed to provide support and guidance, but members are encouraged to be self-reliant as much as reasonably possible (Simms et al, 2013). Although there remain debates about how to develop strong member activism and when and how officers should step in to support members, organizing has become the dominant form of renewal strategy for most unions in the UK, as well as often in other countries too. Broadly, worker-oriented organizing has consistently been demonstrated to be highly effective (McAlevey, 2016), especially when connected to, and informed by, the resource structures of the wider union (Simms, 2007; Simms et al, 2018). However, intensive worker-oriented organizing is expensive and risky for unions, especially in areas of the labour market where small workplaces – or no workplaces – dominate, with high labour turnover and complex work patterns, such as retail, hospitality, social care, delivery work and similar. Unions face a fundamental challenge that the restructuring of the labour market towards these kinds of work, common in the service sector, presents structural challenges to the opportunities for broader renewal. These structural labour market changes are both a function and facilitator of wider changes in capitalism that add to the challenges facing unions.

Keeping up with the changes in capitalism

While it is fair to say that few people predicted the Great Financial Crisis (GFC) of 2008–09, many scholars and commentators had been identifying and theorizing significant shifts in the nature of capitalism through the early 2000s (see Lapavitsas, 2011), with related changes to labour markets, work and employment (Applebaum et al, 2013; Clarke, 2013). The recession following the GFC was unusual because it had relatively small effects on the labour market. Despite negative effects for some groups, in particular, young workers, the widely predicted shedding of labour and resultant uptick in unemployment did not happen (for summary of policy responses, see Clegg, 2010). What did happen was an intensification of the trend towards precarious employment and experimentation with new forms of work, such as work hours being offered through a platform app similar to those used by companies like Uber or Deliveroo. There has also been a decade of very low wage growth, especially in lower-paid jobs.

These changes are indicative of a broader shift in the organization of capital. Here, the term 'financialization' is used to capture the breadth and depth of these changes. Financialization is well theorized elsewhere (for an excellent introduction, see Froud et al, 2006), and with colleagues (Grady and Simms, 2019), I have written elsewhere about how the dynamics of financialization present new challenges for unions in both the UK and beyond. Here, I focus on two crucial developments: first, that the financialization of decision making within organizations makes it difficult for, in the words of Thompson (2003), 'employers to keep their side of the bargain'; and, second, that, at the same time, it is harder – though not impossible – for unions to build the solidarities that are needed to challenge capital in general and managerial decision making specifically.

Thompson (2003, 2011) shows how the privileging of financial priorities within corporate decision making makes it harder for local managers to deliver the commitments necessary to build trust and long-term employment relationships. One example he gives is the way in which financialized decision making often pits groups of workers (perhaps in different plants, offices or countries) against each other for continued investment in their workplaces. He shows how local managers compete for continued investment from the corporate centre, negotiating with workers to increase productivity. However, the continuity of investment is not in the gift of those local managers and can be withdrawn capriciously by often-invisible decision makers, who are incentivized to invest only in the most financially beneficial localities. At the workplace level, this means that local managers have to strike deals with the local union and workforce that they know can be overturned with little notice. Unions have little opportunity to negotiate with the 'real' decision makers, who are often overseas and, in practice, have little interest in workforce-management issues.

This kind of managerial structure and decision making clearly pits groups of workers against each other, whether that is in different workplaces, in different countries or using different work practices. A response by unions could be to focus on building solidarities (expressions of common interests) between workers to unite around a shared negotiation objective. An example that is often used is the work that many unions have done to counter the 'us and them' narrative around migrant workers (Martínez Lucio and Perrett, 2009). Rather than framing migrant workers as labour market disruptors who 'push down wages' or 'take jobs' from other workers, unions can work to frame migrant workers as sharing common interests with existing workers and argue that organizing to negotiate better terms and conditions for all is a necessary and appropriate response. This kind of reframing is harder for unions where interests are more divided. An example is access to pension wealth. It is hard to organize to protect the beneficial terms of some pension schemes if a large majority of workers have only very minimal access to pension provision (for further examples, see Grady and Simms, 2019). Financialization is therefore a far broader phenomenon that affects not only decision making by managers in our workplaces but also our lives, housing conditions, retirement and leisure time.

In this context, unions have to work harder to frame the common interests between, for example, those with housing wealth and those without, as well as those with access to pensions and those with little access. These issues are particularly stark because in the UK, they are, in part, generational.[1] Many workers under the age of around 35 have little opportunity to access housing or pension wealth. They are disproportionately affected by precarity in employment because they are more likely to work in sectors where the disruptive effects of companies like Uber and Deliveroo have spread to competitors.[2]

The future terrain of unions in industrial relations: the centrally important role of the state

Informed in no small part by the initiatives and experiments undertaken in the 1990s and 2000s to refine and expand the craft of organizing, UK unions are in a stronger position to understand what works when they engage workers at the workplace level. However, this leaves open much broader questions about the wider strategies for large-scale renewal. Here, the challenges are much more profound because of the nature of financialized capitalism and the lack of institutional support: it is one thing for organizing workers to seek – and perhaps even win – union recognition in a workplace; it is quite another to sustain regular collective bargaining wins that will ensure the sustainability of union representation in that workplace; and it is an even bigger challenge to then seek to regulate the terms and conditions of employment across the sector or occupation. Those wider objectives are extremely constrained by the landscape of industrial relations. Of particular importance is the role of the state. It is no surprise that capital often seeks to avoid collective negotiation with workers. The moments where the landscape shifts are often when the state chooses to change the terrain of industrial relations institutions to require engagement, often in response to social, political and/or economic crises.

This matters for UK unions in two important ways: first, they seek to use the mechanisms that do exist to challenge the dominance of financialized capital; and, second, there is a broader effort to shift the position of the state towards greater support for a collective worker voice. The good news is that, although small in scale, there is evidence of pressures for both. Unions, including newly emerged independent unions like the Independent Workers Union of Great Britain (IWGB) and United Voices of the World (UVW) (Però, 2020), have used institutions of labour law to challenge some of the financialized and disruptive business models, such as those of Deliveroo and Uber. Specific UK legal challenges have focused on the status of workers as 'workers' rather than self-employed contractors, as workers have specific legal rights to, for example, minimum rates of pay, holiday pay, rest breaks and so on. Licensing regulations have increasingly been an important way to regulate labour markets (Thelen, 2018; Zwick, 2018), and there have been important challenges to the licensing of Uber in specific UK cities (see Amaxopoulou, 2020). These show that there are existing institutions of state regulation (often, though not always, courts) that can be used by unions and others to challenge the emergent business models.

A second approach is to seek to extend state support for the institutions of collective employment regulation. The 2019 Labour Party manifesto picked up on growing arguments for the state to step in to develop systems of sectoral collective bargaining (Labour Party, 2019). Similarly, in Scotland, there have been vocal arguments made to develop and support sectoral bargaining in the social care sector in response to particular problems revealed by the COVID-19 crisis. The Labour Party manifesto pledge has not had an opportunity to progress because the party lost that general election, but it was a bold commitment and it signalled a very profound shift in thinking about industrial relations. The Scottish government has renewed its commitment to seek to introduce sectoral bargaining in the care sector, but the outcome is still uncertain.

These examples are highlighted not because they have yet yielded significant change but because they show that some politicians and policy makers have accepted the analysis that union organizing success will always be constrained when it takes place in a broader landscape of a relatively 'light-touch' approach to employment law and enforcement, as well as an absence of wider institutions of social dialogue and collective bargaining. In such a setting, it is unsurprising that there is a wider debate about the future of work that is noted for its anxiety and dystopianism. If the future is decided without a mechanism for the worker voice to be heard, why would workers not be anxious about that future?

Conclusion

Echoing the point of Müller-Jentsch (1985) that trade unions are 'intermediary organizations', the future of trade unions in the UK will, inevitably, be strongly linked to the future of capitalism, the future of work and the future of institutions of (collective) regulation of employment, but it would be wrong to suggest that unions are passive recipients of these futures. On the contrary, unions are active agents in the structures and processes of industrial relations; they shape those structures and processes as much as they are shaped by them. The attacks of the 1980s and 1990s on those processes and institutions by both the state and employers means that organizing workers one workplace or occupational group at a time is highly unlikely to yield the widespread transformation of employment regulation.

A more profound change can only really come about if institutions of employment regulation (industrial relations) are (re)built. Those institutions are not only workplace bargaining but also labour laws and other legal regulations, such as the NMW, mechanisms to enforce those laws, structures to extend collective bargaining beyond the workplace or occupational group, forums for social dialogue, means of engaging social partners in structures that regulate training, skills and work-related forms of social security, and many other mechanisms that interact to affect the terrain within which the employment relationship takes place. That surely requires intervention from the state. At the UK level, the current dominance of the Conservative Party within Parliament means that there is little likelihood that such a shift of policy will be possible. However, the devolved jurisdictions of Scotland, Wales and Northern Ireland all have a stronger commitment to, and structures of, social dialogue, which may indicate that this is an area where we may see further divergence across the UK.

Notes

[1] For an overview of union strategies to engage with young workers, see Cha et al (2019) and Simms et al (2018).
[2] For an account of the issues of organizing in the gig economy, see Tassinari and Maccarrone (2020).

References

Addison, J.T. and Siebert, W.S. (2003) 'Changes in collective bargaining in the UK', in J.T. Addison and C. Schnabel (eds) *International Handbook of Trade Unions*, Cheltenham: Edward Elgar, pp 415–60.

Amaxopoulou, M. (2020) 'Sticks and carrots: lessons from regulating Uber as a private hire operator in England', *King's Law Journal*, 31(2): 260–74.

Appelbaum, E., Batt, R. and Clark, I. (2013) 'Implications of financial capitalism for employment relations research: evidence from breach of trust and implicit contracts in private equity buyouts', *British Journal of Industrial Relations*, 51(3): 498–518.

BEIS (Department for Business, Energy and Industrial Strategy) (2022) 'Trade union memberships, UK 1995–2021: statistical bulletin'. Available at: https://assets.publishing.service.gov.uk/government/uploads/system/uploads/attachment_data/file/1077904/Trade_Union_Membership_UK_1995-2021_statistical_bulletin.pdf

Brown, W. (1986) 'The changing role of trade unions in the management of labour', *British Journal of Industrial Relations*, 24(2): 161–8.

Bryson, A. and Gomez, R. (2005) 'Why have workers stopped joining unions? The rise in never-membership in Britain', *British Journal of Industrial Relations*, 43: 67–92.

Cha, M., Dupuy, C., Holgate, J., Simms, M. and Tapia, M. (2019) 'Unions are only as old as they feel: lessons on young worker engagement from the UK, France, Germany and the US', ETUI Research Paper – Policy Brief 2/2019, 6 May.

Clark, I. (2013) 'Templates for financial control: management and employee interests under private equity', *Human Resource Management Journal*, 23(2): 144–59.

Clegg, D. (2010) 'Labour market policy in the crisis: the UK in comparative perspective', *Journal of Poverty and Social Justice*, 18(1): 5–17.

Cumbers, A. (2005) 'Genuine renewal or pyrrhic victory? The scale politics of trade union recognition in the UK', *Antipode*, 37(1): 116–38.

Dickens, L. and Hall, M. (2003) 'Labour law and industrial relations: a new settlement?', in P.K. Edwards (ed) *Industrial Relations: Theory and Practice*, Oxford: Blackwell, pp 124–56.

Froud, J., Johal, S., Leaver, A. and Williams, K. (2006) *Financialization and Strategy: Narrative and Numbers*, London and New York: Routledge.

Grady, J. and Simms, M. (2019) 'Trade unions and the challenge of fostering solidarities in an era of financialisation', *Economic and Industrial Democracy*, 40(3): 490–510.

Heery, E. and Simms, M. (2008) 'Constraints on union organising in the United Kingdom', *Industrial Relations Journal*, 39(1): 24–42.

Labour Party (2019) 'Labour Party manifesto'. Available at: https://labour.org.uk/wp-content/uploads/2019/11/Real-Change-Labour-Manifesto-2019.pdf

Lapavitsas, C. (2011) 'Theorizing financialization', *Work, Employment and Society*, 25(4): 611–26.

Machin, S. (1997) 'The decline of labour market institutions and the rise in wage inequality in Britain', *European Economic Review*, 41(3–5): 647–57.

Martínez Lucio, M. and Perrett, R. (2009) 'The diversity and politics of trade unions' responses to minority ethnic and migrant workers: the context of the UK', *Economic and Industrial Democracy*, 30(3): 324–47.

McAlevey, J.F. (2016) *No Shortcuts: Organizing for Power in the New Gilded Age*, Oxford: Oxford University Press.

McIlroy, J. (1998) 'The enduring alliance? Trade unions and the making of New Labour, 1994–1997', *British Journal of Industrial Relations*, 36: 537–64.

Müller-Jentsch, W. (1985) 'Trade unions as intermediary organizations', *Economic and Industrial Democracy*, 6(1): 3–33.

ONS (Office for National Statistics) (2023) 'Labour market overview, UK: February 2023'. Available at: www.ons.gov.uk/employmentandlabou rmarket/peopleinwork/employmentandemployeetypes/bulletins/uklabou rmarket/february2023

Però, D. (2020) 'Indie unions, organizing and labour renewal: learning from precarious migrant workers', *Work, Employment and Society*, 34(5): 900–18.

Schott, K. (1982) 'The rise of Keynesian economics: Britain 1940–64', *Economy and Society*, 11(3): 292–316.

Simms, M. (2007) 'Managed activism: two union organising campaigns in the not-for-profit sector', *Industrial Relations Journal*, 38(2): 119–35.

Simms, M., Holgate, J. and Heery, E. (2013) *Union Voices: Tensions and Tactics in UK Organizing*, Ithaca, NY: Cornell University Press.

Simms, M., Eversberg, D., Dupuy, C. and Hipp, L. (2018) 'Organizing young workers under precarious conditions: what hinders or facilitates union success', *Work and Occupations*, 45(4): 420–50.

Smith, P. and Morton, G. (2006) 'Nine years of New Labour: neoliberalism and workers' rights', *British Journal of Industrial Relations*, 44(3): 401–20.

Tassinari, A. and Maccarrone, V. (2020) 'Riders on the storm: workplace solidarity among gig economy couriers in Italy and the UK', *Work, Employment and Society*, 34(1): 35–54.

Thelen, K. (2018) 'Regulating Uber: the politics of the platform economy in Europe and the United States', *Perspectives on Politics*, 16(4): 938–53.

Thompson, P. (2003) 'Disconnected capitalism: or why employers can't keep their side of the bargain', *Work, Employment and Society*, 17(2): 359–78.

Thompson, P. (2011) 'The trouble with HRM', *Human Resource Management Journal*, 21(4): 355–67.

Waddington, J. (2019) 'United Kingdom: a long-term assault on collective bargaining', in T. Muller, K. Vandaele and J. Waddington (eds) *Collective Bargaining in Europe: Towards an Endgame*, Brussels: ETUI, pp 605–24.

Zwick, A. (2018) 'Welcome to the gig economy: neoliberal industrial relations and the case of Uber', *GeoJournal*, 83: 679–91.

6

Expanding the Boundaries of Industrial Relations as a Field of Study: The Role of 'New Actors'

Steve Williams

Work on so-called 'new actors' in industrial relations (Heery and Frege, 2006; Cooke and Wood, 2014) has not only added to our knowledge and understanding of industrial relations but also highlighted its distinctiveness and vitality as a field of study, and expanded its boundaries. But what do we mean by an industrial relations 'actor'? Influenced by Dunlop's (1958) concept of an 'industrial relations system', the field was traditionally dominated by a concern with understanding collective relations between workers, represented by trade unions, and employers, often organized in employers' associations (Heery and Frege, 2006). The label 'new' can thus be applied to actors – individuals, organizations, institutions and movements – that either did not used to have much of a role in industrial relations or did have one but were neglected.

Much of the credit for stimulating a greater concern with new actors must go to Bellemare (2000). His study of the Canadian city of Montreal showed the important influence over industrial relations exercised by public transport users. The work of bus drivers, for example, was affected in some important ways by the attitudes and expectations of passengers. Bellemare's (2000) principal theoretical contribution was to conceptualize the nature of an industrial relations actor based on the extent of their involvement at three levels – the workplace, the organization and wider society, respectively – and their impact. Further studies of 'end users' in health and social care highlight their importance as actors in industrial relations. For example, the activities of patients' representatives can influence how individual staff are managed in hospital settings (Bellemare et al, 2018).

Moreover, empowering users of care services has important implications for how carers' work is organized (Kessler and Bach, 2011). However, Bellemare's (2000) approach, with its emphasis on being influential at all three levels and the continuity of such influence, is perhaps too restrictive, potentially excluding actors who play an important part in industrial relations but whose involvement is restricted to a single level or is intermittent (Abbott, 2006; Kessler and Bach, 2011).

In the case of certain actors, it is not that they are necessarily 'new' but rather that their role has become more prominent or better understood. Some examples are as follows. John Logan (2006) detailed the important contribution made by anti-union law firms and consultants to corporate efforts to suppress unionization in the US. The role of law firms in industrial relations in the UK has also attracted greater scrutiny, particularly the part some play in litigating on behalf of women workers with equal pay claims in areas like local government and supermarket retailing (Beirne and Wilson, 2016).

By supplying labour on a temporary basis, employment agencies have long offered employers greater numerical flexibility (Forde, 2001). Yet, there is a growing understanding of the important role of agencies in enabling certain groups of workers, such as migrant workers, who might otherwise struggle to get jobs, to find employment (Hopkins and Dawson, 2016). In so doing, agencies play an increasingly prominent part in industrial relations, not only as labour market intermediaries but also in constructing markets and how they are regulated (MacKenzie and Martínez Lucio, 2019: 189). In some areas of the economy, particularly in retail, distribution and logistics, employers use agency labour in a 'strategic' manner, not only as a means of filling short-term vacancies or responding to unexpected surges in demand but also as a fundamental feature of a business model that privileges business flexibility at the expense of workers' job security (Briken and Taylor, 2018; Resolution Foundation, 2018).

Strictly speaking, law firms and employment agencies are not 'new' actors; however, the nature and importance of their activities in industrial relations are now better appreciated and understood. There are also actors whose role has become more prominent. In the US, for example, private employment arbitrators have become widely used for the purpose of settling individual employment disputes. Large non-unionized firms often use clauses in employment contracts to prohibit staff from litigating over alleged breaches of their employment rights and prescribe mandatory private arbitration (Seeber and Lipsky, 2006; Colvin, 2016).

One type of actor that is more clearly 'new' in respect of industrial relations, though, is the employers' forum model. Employers' associations have long had a prominent role in industrial relations, even if their traditional focus on joint regulation has largely been superseded by an emphasis on advice, consultancy and lobbying activities (Gooberman et al, 2019). During the 2000s and 2010s, though, new collective organizations of employers developed, often called 'forums', particularly for the purpose of representing business interests in respect of equality and diversity matters. The emphasis on voluntary standard setting, as exemplified by the activity of such organizations as the Business Disability Forum (BDF), is characteristic of the growing influence of a corporate social responsibility (CSR) approach on management practice among leading employers (Gooberman et al, 2018).

The rise of a CSR approach has clearly affected the management of industrial relations in some important respects, as the activities of employers' forums like the BDF indicate. However, the process of financialization, characterized by the increasing influence of international bond markets, private equity and pension funds (Batt, 2018), has had a more profound impact on the management of employment relations, particularly in liberal market economies, such as the US and UK. One important consequence of the rise of what Dundon and Rafferty (2018) call 'investor capitalism' is an emphasis on short-term, cost-minimization measures that compromise managerial efforts to build employee engagement. Importantly, though, efforts to build greater dialogue between major international financial institutions, such as the World Bank and the International Monetary Fund, and the global trade union movement are designed to encourage the development of a social dimension to the structure of global governance (Rueckert, 2021).

All this shows how the activities of new actors, or established actors whose role has become more prominent or better understood, have influenced the management of industrial relations. Yet, the work of new actors, particularly civil society organizations (CSOs), such as pressure groups, advocacy bodies, social movement organizations and community organizations, is predominantly concerned with supporting, representing and advancing the interests of workers, albeit generally without being involved in bargaining on their behalf (Heery et al, 2012a).

There are five main ways in which CSOs act on behalf of working people. One approach involves efforts to organize workers, operating as 'quasi-unions' (Heckscher and Carré, 2006), generally from outside of workplaces and beyond the boundaries of employing organizations. In the US, the term 'alt-labour' describes organizations like community-based worker centres that organize and advocate on behalf of workers, for example, supporting litigation against employers (Fine, 2006; Eidelson, 2013). Generally, alt-labour organizations do not seek to engage in collective bargaining activity with employers, something that distinguishes them from conventional labour unions. Yet, not only have US unions sought to forge greater collaborations with alt-labour themselves but some have also developed their own alt-labour organizing initiatives (Milkman and Ott, 2014).

US-style alt-labour organizations have become established in the UK, including the Independent Workers Union of Great Britain (IWGB) and United Voices of the World (UVW). While formally – and legally – operating as trade unions, they put a greater emphasis on grass-roots activism than is conventionally the case with more established unions. The IWGB and UVW are particularly concerned with representing, organizing and mobilizing workers in precarious forms of employment, such as those working for online labour platforms or as contract cleaners, using a combination of litigation and direct action, including protests, though often with the aim of bargaining collectively with employing organizations (Cant, 2020). In China, where independent trade unions are prohibited, labour non-governmental organizations (NGOs) have become more involved in organizing workers collectively, contributing to a nascent independent labour movement (Li and Liu, 2018).

The second approach used by CSOs to support and promote the interests of working people involves providing workers with services. Public-interest legal organizations, charities and voluntary organizations, such as the network of Citizens' Advice Bureaux (CABs) in the UK, provide workers with information, advice and guidance about employment rights and protections, and sometimes support for litigation against employers who are alleged to have breached workers' statutory employment rights and protections (Abbott, 2006). In principle, the services provided by CABs should be especially valuable for vulnerable, non-unionized workers, including minority ethnic and migrant workers, who lack alternative sources of support. In practice, however, accessing CAB services is by no means straightforward, and the advice on offer is often inadequate, resulting in workers having to be referred to more specialist bodies, such as law centres (Holgate et al, 2012; Kirk, 2018).

Charities and professional movement organizations provide workers with information, advice and support about specific employment-related issues. In the UK, for example, disability organizations like the Epilepsy Society and Scope are regarded by disabled graduates as 'legitimate sources of knowledge and information, not only about legislation but also societal and medical issues' (William and Cunningham, 2021: 661). They also provide labour market services, in the form of schemes that facilitate disabled workers' access to employment and their career progression (William and Cunningham 2021). Some CSOs offer mentoring services, for example, targeted at women workers (Heery and Williams, 2020). In the US, the Freelancers' Union provides independent contractors with financial benefits and professional development and networking opportunities, not only out of a concern with providing services but also based on the belief that encouraging greater mutuality can be empowering (King, 2014; Fine, 2015).

The third way in which CSOs seek to support and promote the interests of working people involves efforts to influence public policy in industrial relations, largely through campaigning and lobbying interventions concerned with improving workers' rights and protections that are directed at the state. In the US, for example, living-wage campaigns are often concerned with inducing cities and municipalities to establish local ordinances regulating low pay (Luce, 2004). In the UK, CSOs' industrial relations activities often involve efforts to engage with the state, based on the belief that persuading policy makers of the need for change over such matters as encouraging flexible working, supporting working carers, protecting vulnerable workers and tackling disadvantage and discrimination in employment is desirable (Williams et al, 2017). One key feature of CSOs' efforts in this area concerns their claim to offer expert-based advocacy, based on their specialist knowledge of a specific policy area (Williams and Abbott, 2019). Maternity Action, for example, lobbies vigorously against pregnancy discrimination and to improve pregnancy and maternity rights and protections at work, informed by the expertise it has accrued in this particular area and the experiences of the women with whom it works (Maternity Action, 2013).

The fourth approach used by CSOs to support the interests of workers involves efforts to engage directly with employing organizations for the purpose of improving the management of people at work. Perhaps the most prominent example of such 'civil regulation' in the UK concerns the activity of the Living Wage Foundation (LWF). It operates an accreditation scheme for those employers who pledge to pay their staff and indirect workers employed by their contractors a 'real' living wage. The LWF looks to engage positively with employers, highlighting the business benefits that supposedly arise from pursuing an ethical approach to managing people at work. Its work 'is directed primarily at employers and is overwhelmingly positive in orientation, appealing to employers to join its campaign to tackle in-work poverty and recognizing their contribution when they do so' (Heery et al, 2017: 807). By 2022, the LWF had accredited around 9,000 'living-wage employers', including major banks, such as Barclays, Lloyds and HSBC, an impressive achievement given that the accreditation programme was only established in 2011.

The fifth way in which CSOs intervene in industrial relations in support of workers' interests is through community-based organizing and mobilizing efforts, often in coalitions encompassing trade unions. There is some good evidence that mobilization by community-based organizations and movements can benefit working people (McBride and Greenwood, 2009). The living-wage movement in the UK, for example, originated and developed from coalition working between community bodies, faith groups and trade unions (Wills, 2008).

What makes mobilization efforts by community-based organizations and networks distinctive? The experience of the UK-based Latin American Workers Association (LAWAS) suggests that two features are pertinent.

One is an emphasis on grass-roots activism led by working people themselves, such as migrant workers, who are rooted in specific communities. A second feature concerns the connections made between migrant workers' objective experiences of exploitative working conditions and their subjective identities as individuals with distinctive backgrounds and lived experiences (Alberti and Però, 2018). Evidence from Israel demonstrates that effective coalition working between community-based organizations and trade unions can improve the working lives of outsourced and subcontracted workers (Preminger, 2018).

Yet, there are some important obstacles that prevent effective joint working between community-based CSOs and trade unions. The LAWAS, for example, struggled to get union support for its mobilization on behalf of migrant workers (Alberti and Però, 2018). The 'relational' culture evident in community organizations and networks, characterized by flexibility and informality, can conflict with the 'instrumental' rationality based on formal and bureaucratic administrative systems that often prevails in trade unions (Tapia, 2013). Moreover, community-based organization and mobilization have their own specific weaknesses, including a sometimes rather naive belief in the effectiveness of business-case arguments for driving improvements in people's working lives and the lack of a presence within the workplace (Alberti, 2016).

In addition to the approaches characterized here, there is also an important transnational dimension to the activities of CSOs when it comes to protecting, supporting and advancing the interests of working people, stimulated by the greater global interconnectedness associated with globalization. The work of international advocacy organizations, particularly those concerned with human rights, often encompasses labour rights' issues. Amnesty International, for example, has publicized labour abuses on construction projects for the 2022 men's football World Cup in Qatar and has exhorted the Qatari government and football authorities to make improvements (Amnesty International, 2019). Social movement organizations and networks, such as the international Clean Clothes Campaign in the garment industry, play an important part in campaigning and mobilizing support for improved labour standards in global supply chains (Balsiger, 2014). CSOs are also involved in multi-stakeholder initiatives designed to regulate labour standards on a transnational basis. The Accord for Fire and Safety in Bangladesh, a five-year, legally binding agreement between global brands, retailers and trade union organizations, established in response to the 2013 Rana Plaza factory collapse, when over 1,100 people died, includes social movement organizations like the Clean Clothes Campaign as 'witness signatories' (Reinecke and Donaghey, 2015).

In conclusion, there are three key insights to be derived from this review of new actors in industrial relations. First, while some of the actors concerned are not necessarily all that new but, rather, may previously have been neglected, work on CSOs, in particular, demonstrates that the involvement of new actors, generally outside of workplaces, became more important during the 2000s and 2010s. Second, the attention received by new actors highlights the distinctiveness of industrial relations – the concern with workers' interests and the potential for conflict in, and the regulation of, work and employment relationships – its vitality and its importance as a field of study. Third, and perhaps most importantly, the greater knowledge and understanding of industrial relations derived from studies of new actors reflects a broadening of the field to encompass contemporary topics, such as globalization, consumption relations (Donaghey et al, 2014), financialization (Dundon and Rafferty, 2018) and CSR (Heery et al, 2017). The growing concern with new actors is also a function of changes in the nature of the industrial relations field itself in a more neoliberalized setting, with issues like low pay, employment discrimination and precarity coming to the fore (Heery, 2016). CSOs are often concerned with supporting workers who are vulnerable or who are at particular risk of being disadvantaged in some way, such as disabled workers (William and Cunningham, 2021). In contributing to re-regulatory pressures in industrial relations, CSOs' interventions tend to complement, rather than supplant, trade union representation (Heery et al, 2012b) and should be understood on their own terms (Williams and Abbott, 2019). The increased activity of CSOs often reflects changing political opportunity structures; for example, the expansion of individual employment law has prompted actors with specialist interests and expertise, such as disability charities, to become more involved in efforts to influence work and employment relationships (Heery et al, 2012a). All this highlights the continued importance of industrial relations as a field of study, as its boundaries have expanded, not least because of the activities of the 'new' actors covered in this chapter.

References

Abbott, B. (2006) 'Determining the significance of the Citizens Advice Bureau as an industrial relations actor', *Employee Relations*, 28(5): 435–48.

Alberti, G. (2016) 'Moving beyond the dichotomy of workplace and community unionism: the challenges of organising migrant workers in London's hotels', *Economic and Industrial Democracy*, 37(1): 73–94.

Alberti, G. and Però, D. (2018) 'Migrating industrial relations: migrant workers' initiative within and without trade unions', *British Journal of Industrial Relations*, 56(4): 693–715.

Amnesty International (2019) 'Qatar reality check: the state of migrant workers' rights with four years to go until the Qatar 2022 World Cup'. Available at: www.amnesty.org/en/latest/campaigns/2019/02/reality-check-migrant-workers-rights-with-four-years to qatar-2022-world-cup/

Balsiger, P. (2014) *The Fight for Ethical Fashion. The Origins and Interactions of the Clean Clothes Movement*, Farnham: Ashgate.

Batt, R. (2018) 'The financial model of the firm, the "future of work", and employment relations', in A. Wilkinson, T. Dundon, J. Donaghey and A. Colvin (eds) *The Routledge Companion to Employment Relations*, Abingdon: Routledge, pp 465–79.

Beirne, M. and Wilson, F. (2016) 'Running with "wolves" or waiting for a happy release? Evaluating routes to gender equality', *Work, Employment and Society*, 30(2): 220–36.

Bellemare, G. (2000) 'End users: actors in the industrial relations system', *British Journal of Industrial Relations*, 38(3): 383–405.

Bellemare, G., Briand, L., Havard, C. and Naschberger, C. (2018) 'Users/patients as industrial relations actors: a structurationist analysis', *Relations Industrielles*, 73(3): 486–516.

Briken, K. and Taylor, P. (2018) 'Fulfilling the "British way": beyond constrained choice – Amazon workers' lived experiences of workfare', *Industrial Relations Journal*, 49(5–6): 438–58.

Cant, C. (2020) *Riding for Deliveroo: Resistance in the New Economy*, Cambridge: Polity.

Colvin, A. (2016) 'Conflict and employment relations in the individual rights era', in D. Lipsky, A. Avgar and R. Lamare (eds) *Managing and Resolving Workplace Conflict (Advances in Industrial and Labor Relations, Volume 22)*, Bingley: Emerald, pp 1–30.

Cooke, F.-L. and Wood, G. (2014) 'New actors in employment relations', in A. Wilkinson, G. Wood and R. Deeg (eds) *The Oxford Handbook of Employment Relations: Comparative Employment Systems*, Oxford: Oxford University Press, pp 683–700.

Donaghey, J., Reinecke, J., Niforou, C. and Lawson, B. (2014) 'From employment relations to consumption relations: balancing labour governance in global supply chains', *Human Resource Management*, 53(2): 229–52.

Dundon, T. and Rafferty, A. (2018) 'The (potential) demise of HRM?', *Human Resource Management Journal*, 28(3): 377–91.

Dunlop, J. (1958) *Industrial Relations Systems*, New York: Holt.

Eidelson, J. (2013) 'Alt-labor', *The American Prospect*, 29 January. Available at: https://prospect.org/notebook/alt-labor/

Fine, J. (2006) *Worker Centers: Organising Communities at the Edge of the Dream*, Ithaca, NY: ILR Press.

Fine, J. (2015) 'Alternative labour protection movements in the United States: reshaping industrial relations?', *International Labour Review*, 154(1): 15–26.

Forde, C. (2001) 'Temporary arrangements: the activities of employment agencies in the UK', *Work, Employment and Society*, 15(3): 631–44.

Gooberman, L., Hauptmeier, M. and Heery, E. (2018) 'Contemporary employer interest representation in the United Kingdom', *Work, Employment and Society*, 32(1): 114–32.

Gooberman, L., Hauptmeier, M. and Heery, E. (2019) 'The decline of employers' associations in the UK, 1976–2014', *Journal of Industrial Relations*, 61(1): 11–32.

Hecksher, C. and Carré, F. (2006) 'Strength in networks: employment rights organisations and the problem of co-ordination', *British Journal of Industrial Relations*, 44(4): 605–28.

Heery, E. (2016) 'British industrial relations pluralism in the era of neo-liberalism', *Journal of Industrial Relations*, 58(1): 3–24.

Heery, E. and Frege, C. (2006) 'New actors in industrial relations', *British Journal of Industrial Relations*, 44(4): 601–4.

Heery, E. and Williams, S. (2020) 'Civil society organizations and employee voice', in A. Wilkinson, J. Donaghey, T. Dundon and R. Freeman (eds) *Handbook of Research on Employee Voice*, 2nd edn, Cheltenham: Edward Elgar, pp 202–21.

Heery, E., Abbott, B. and Williams, S. (2012a) 'The involvement of civil society organisations in British industrial relations: extent, origins, significance', *British Journal of Industrial Relations*, 50(1): 47–72.

Heery, E., Williams, S. and Abbott, B. (2012b) 'Civil society organisations and trade unions: cooperation, conflict, indifference', *Work, Employment and Society*, 26(1): 145–60.

Heery, E., Hann, D. and Nash, D. (2017) 'The Living Wage campaign in the UK'. *Employee Relations*, 39(6): 800–14.

Holgate, J., Pollert, A., Keles, J. and Kumarappan, L. (2012) 'De-collectivization and employment problems: the experiences of minority ethnic workers seeking help through Citizens Advice', *Work, Employment and Society*, 26(5): 772–878.

Hopkins, B. and Dawson, C. (2016) 'Migrant workers and involuntary non-permanent jobs: agencies as new IR actors?', *Industrial Relations Journal*, 47(2): 163–80.

Kessler, I. and Bach, S. (2011) 'The citizen-consumer as industrial relations actor: new ways of working and the end-user in social care', *British Journal of Industrial Relations*, 49(1): 80–102.

King, M. (2014) 'Protecting and representing workers in the new gig economy. The case of the Freelancers Union', in R. Milkman and E. Ott (eds) *New Labour in New York: Precarious Workers and the Future of the Labour Movement*, Ithaca, NY, and London: ILR Press, pp 150–70.

Kirk, E. (2018) 'The "problem" with the employment tribunal system: reform, rhetoric, and realities for the clients of Citizens' Advice Bureaux', *Work, Employment and Society*, 32(6): 975–91.

Li, C. and Liu, M. (2018) 'Overcoming collective action problems facing Chinese workers: lessons from four protests against Walmart', *Industrial and Labor Relations Review*, 71(5): 1078–105.

Logan, J. (2006) 'The union avoidance industry in the United States', *British Journal of Industrial Relations*, 44(4): 651–75.

Luce, S. (2004) *Fighting for a Living Wage*, Ithaca, NY: Cornell University Press.

MacKenzie, R. and Martínez Lucio, M. (2019) 'Regulation, migration and the implications for industrial relations', *Journal of Industrial Relations*, 61(2): 176–97.

Maternity Action (2013) 'Overdue: a plan of action to tackle pregnancy discrimination now'. Available at: https://maternityaction.org.uk/2013/12/overdue-a-plan-of-action-to-tackle-pregnancy-discrimination-now/

McBride, J. and Greenwood, I. (eds) (2009) *Community Unionism: A Comparative Analysis of Concepts and Contexts*, Basingstoke: Palgrave Macmillan.

Milkman, R. and Ott, E. (eds) (2014) *New Labor in New York. Precarious Workers and the Future of the Labor Movement*, Ithaca, NY: Cornell University Press.

Preminger, J. (2018) 'Creating a multilayered representational "package" for subcontracted workers: the case of cleaners at Ben-Gurion University', *Industrial Relations Journal*, 49(1): 24–49.

Reinecke, J. and Donaghey, J. (2015) 'After Rana Plaza: building coalitional power for labour rights between unions and (consumption-based) social movement organisations', *Organization*, 22(5): 720–40.

Resolution Foundation (2018) 'Parts of British business have become "agency worker reliant" in recent years', 10 February. Available at: https://www.resolutionfoundation.org/press-releases/parts-of-british-business-have-become-agency-worker-reliant-in-recent-years/

Rubery, J. (2011) 'Reconstruction amid deconstruction: or why we need more of the social in European social models', *Work, Employment and Society*, 25(4): 658–74.

Rueckert, Y. (2021) 'The global unions and global governance: analysing the dialogue between the international trade union organizations and the international financial institutions', *Economic and Industrial Democracy*, 42(3): 766–84.

Seeber, R. and Lipsky, D. (2006) 'The ascendancy of employment arbitrators in US employment relations: a new actor in the American system?', *British Journal of Industrial Relations*, 44(4): 719–56.

Tapia, M. (2013) 'Marching to different tunes: commitment and culture as mobilizing mechanisms of trade unions and community organizations', *British Journal of Industrial Relations*, 51(4): 666–88.

William, L. and Cunningham, I. (2021) 'Evaluating the role of trade unions and civil society organizations in supporting graduate educated disabled employees', *Economic and Industrial Democracy*, 42(3): 648–66.

Williams, S. and Abbott, B. (2019) 'Beyond the workplace: how civil society organizations attempt to exercise regulatory influence over work and employment', in G. Gall (ed) *Handbook of the Politics of Work, Labour, and Employment*, Cheltenham: Edward Elgar, pp 242–60.

Williams, S., Abbott, B. and Heery, E. (2017) 'Civil governance in work and employment relations: how civil society organizations contribute to systems of labour governance', *Journal of Business Ethics*, 144(1): 103–19.

Wills, J. (2008) 'Making class politics possible: organising contract cleaners in London', *International Journal of Urban and Regional Research*, 32(2): 305–23.

7

The State and Industrial Relations: Debates, Concerns and Contradictions in the Forging of Regulatory Change in the UK

Miguel Martínez Lucio and Robert MacKenzie

Introduction

The role of the state in the UK has been the subject of extensive discussion within the industrial relations literature. All states, to some extent, have their idiosyncrasies; however, the historical fault lines and the progressive fragmentation of the state in the UK are curious characteristics, the consequences of which have become clearer in a context of increasing neoliberalism and labour market fragmentation. Yet, what is noticeable are the fundamental contradictions and tensions in the economic and social remits of the state – something that industrial relations scholars have studied and highlighted across a range of issues. As discussed later, much of the debate that engages with the changing nature of the state does not explicitly frame itself in terms of 'the state'; however, it does form an interesting set of insights about the contradictory and ongoing interventionist nature of the state in the UK. The chapter will show how the debate on the state has been key to industrial relations in various ways, though not always in an explicit manner. Furthermore, different periods of debate within industrial relations have captured the changing character of the state, as explored later. More recently, there has been increasing attention paid to the way in which the state has remained a significant factor in the context of a greater emphasis on marketization and what is often labelled 'neoliberalism', albeit in a decentred and increasingly contradictory fashion. The contribution of industrial relations academics to the debate on the state is therefore more engaging than first meets the eye, partly because the discipline has always been concerned with addressing some of the more informal and discreet features of regulation.

The problem of the UK state: trust and industrial relations autonomy

Keeping the state out of the direct regulation of worker representation and collective action has been a mainstream characteristic of UK industrial relations – supported by organized labour and capital – since the early 20th century. Recent work by Dorey (2019) on the then Labour government's attempts to reform industrial conflict and worker representation in the 1960s shows us how strong the defence of an autonomous sphere of worker representation was in shaping the debate on the state's reach, even as intervention was increasing elsewhere in terms of welfare and health services. The debate within pluralist circles was very much focused on questions of reforming and formalizing the nature of labour relations, especially the central and pivotal role of collective bargaining (Clegg, 1976; Ackers, 2007). Consensus around welfare reform and intervention was, in great part, separate to the role the state should play in industrial relations, not only due to the legacy of worker representation and its development but also due to the historic distrust trade unionists had of the state's role within the workplace. Brief forays into the debates on corporatism from radical perspectives within both political studies and industrial relations seemed to highlight the risks of engaging with the state (Panitch, 1981). Moreover, even with its relatively more structured mechanisms of representation and the narrative of the public sector as a 'good' employer (see Winchester, 1983), the state was, for some, never systematic in its concerns with 'fairness' at work (Hyman, 1975; Hyman and Brough, 1975). Much of the debate regarding the state was focused on the difficulties of generating effective structures of regulation and dialogue, especially as it entered a crisis context. Nevertheless, even during the ensuing crisis of the Keynesian welfare state, the late 1970s tends to be forgotten as a moment of reform in terms of gender and race equality, the increasing role of legal redress, and the formalizing of health-and-safety rights. However, this must be set against the early 1970s' statutory attempts at reforming industrial relations and the use of the courts to curtail collective voice, as seen with the 'Shrewsbury 24' (see Darlington and Lyddon, 2001; Turnbull, 2022). The role of covert state departments and the security services in influencing the trial in Shrewsbury of 24 building workers also raises issues regarding the 'hidden state', which are once again coming to the fore. The failure of social democracy in the 1960s and 1970s to 'modernize' industrial relations through the state, or to create a stronger pattern of collective worker voice and influence (which are not the same thing for some in the discipline), led to the opening of the political space to more belligerent policies and discourses of 'reform'. This period heralded a more ambivalent social and political context of new struggles.

The state and the New Right

With the election of the New Right Conservative government in 1979, we see the emergence of a more coercive and directly interventionist state on matters of collective rights and worker voice. Simultaneously, an increasing fascination with the way the state was understood began to make its presence felt. In some senses, the state was being curtailed, for example, in terms of the direct social and welfare role it was to play, and notably in the national ownership of key parts of industry. The state was also intent on reforming the space of worker representation by restricting the range of rights on collective action and, indeed, the governance of trade unions. The miners' strike of 1984–85 saw the deployment of a more directly interventionist state that organized its policing and intelligence services in novel ways (see Beynon, 1985). This moment of state intervention around restrictive laws and new forms of policing, linked to a new set of financial elites 'globalizing' the national economy, seemed to conform to a view of the British state (as depicted by Miliband [1970]) in terms of social and political elites framing and closing political debate.

During this period, we witness a growing range of studies pointing to the contradictions within this moment – something that seems more obvious from the vantage point of 2022. From some perspectives, this period was contradictory (as outlined by Hall [1988]), as it was both 'authoritarian' and 'populist': the state using particular forms of surveillance and control over a collective labour movement and cultures while highlighting 'individual' progress and market identities. This curious paradox was, in some senses, echoed by Gamble (1988), when he spoke of the link between 'marketization' and a 'strong state' that was pushing this project. In terms of broader developments, Clark (1996) focused on the growing complexity of the state in a context of greater deregulation and 'flexible' labour markets – a process underpinned historically by the uneven nature of industrial development, combined with a history of laissez faire economics and financialization (Clark, 2000).

A state at war with itself? Contradictions and ironies in the development of the state

It is the ambivalence and contradictions associated with the state in the UK that many in the industrial relations discipline started picking up and reflecting on, notably, in relation to specific roles of the state and how they have been changing since the 1980s. This led to work on locating the state in terms of the contradictions between new forms of intervention emerging, notwithstanding the broad 'neoliberal' development of political economy during this period. As the field of industrial relations increasingly interacted with labour-process approaches, the role of the state often lapsed into being an authoritarian prop to a context of supporting greater work intensification. The state blended into the background as the focus fell on the behaviour and intentions of management within the workplace, in a context of greater individualized forms of control and the declining presence of collective worker voice. Even so, there were various streams of analysis emerging that began pointing to the curious tensions and ironies in the way the state 'reconfigured' itself or was reconfigured in the face of competing social and economic developments. These are the sets of themes around which industrial relations scholars began to review the nature of the UK state and its changing as well as contradictory roles.

First, a broad body of studies began pointing out how proactive the state had to become in securing a restructuring of British capitalism, especially in the form of inward investment. The development of an investment arm of the state and more directed forms of intervention related to inward investors – especially Japanese capital during the 1980s and 1990s – was crucial to studies noting the way new ways of 'flexible' working and surveillance-driven management systems were facilitated, and how the local state enabled these processes (Garrahan and Stewart, 1992). In promoting an individualized form of employment relations and constraining collective frameworks, key actors within the state were entrusted with facilitating the entrance of new forms of employer, with their alternative organizational paradigms. The state also created a framework of management learning that used these new points of reference as a way of de-collectivizing industrial relations, contributing to a form of colonization of employment relations by employers (MacKenzie and Martínez Lucio, 2014).

Second, debate emerged over the supply-side roles of the state in relation to training and learning as part of the push towards a general strategy that steadily facilitated the development of a more flexible workforce. The emphasis on soft skills, adaptability and emotional labour formed an important part of the repertoire of vocational education and labour market inclusion programmes (Grugulis, 2006; Stuart, 2007). This dimension of state intervention was increasingly developed with a view to ensuring a greater degree of individualization and flexibility in the labour market. Many academics working on these developments were keen to show that the emergence of such a form of labour market ironically required a proactive state at various levels within the educational sphere. These developments also overlapped with discussions on the engagement of trade unions with state funding and the possibilities and risks of such approximation with the state on such activities as training (Rainbird and Stuart, 2011; McIlroy and Croucher, 2013).

Third, this facilitating dimension of the state has been the subject of a range of interventions outlining the way employers – and, even, trade unions – are prompted into acquiring specific forms of behaviour and practices. During the last Labour administration, government-sponsored projects sustained the development of new forms of social dialogue around partnership, addressed the way in which notions of the 'model employer' were understood and even targeted the internal 'modernization' of trade unions (Martínez Lucio and Stuart, 2011). The continuing centrality of the Advisory Conciliation and Arbitration Service (as well as other bodies, such as the Health and Safety Executive or Equalities and Human Rights Commission) as an organization with an increasing role in strategically guiding economic actors in relation to employment relations has increasingly been seen as part of a consultancy or benchmarking state (Martínez Lucio and Stuart, 2011).

This attempt to legitimate or soften – depending on your point of view – the move to a greater neoliberal market orientation within the country can also be seen at the subnational level, with local councils being supported (or at least not systematically opposed) in their development of employment charters and socially oriented procurement strategies, which attempt to establish 'good employment' benchmarks for employers to pursue. Local state engagement with the notion of the living wage pre-dates the more voluntaristic and symbolic interest taken by the recent Conservative governments (see Johnson, 2017). The rethinking of the local space and the emergence of soft regulation and labour market inclusion strategies have been noticeable as ways to counter some of the harder and excessive consequences of deregulation and labour market fragmentation. Hence, the different spheres of the state and its different levels appear to engage with work and employment in quite diverse ways – though whether this is a deliberate attempt to recreate a more inclusive and social approach to the role of the state is another matter (Yates and Clark, 2018). Moreover, it can lead to a more disorganized system of regulation that undermines or limits the role of collective bargaining (Grimshaw et al, 2017).

In many respects, the state remains a complex entity. Within the public sector – once known as a more modernized and coordinated dimension of the state in terms of its employment relations – we have seen the move to a more decentred management system of joint regulation and 'flexible' employment practices. Yet, ironically, at the same time, greater attention has been paid to new forms of dialogue and joint initiatives around questions of well-being and equality at work. The literature on public sector industrial relations change is extensive in its coverage of the tensions between market and social imperatives within the broad spectrum of 'modernization' (see Bach, 2002). It is noticeable that at the local state level, or through specific state agencies, attempts are being made to mitigate certain aspects of change with social and equality initiatives. However, how extensive these efforts are and the degree to which they are merely symbolic is a matter for discussion, even where there is a more progressive, left-leaning leadership (Byrne, 2018). There is a detectable tension and uncertainty even within expansive programmes of outsourcing and commercialization, as some organizations within the public sector feel an obligation to pull back and ensure certain aspects of the 'good employer'.

Fourth, contradictory developments are noticeable in the question of rights at the individual level, where we have seen a growing interest in the rethinking of such issues as equality. The spaces of individual legal rights and the local dimension of the judiciary has become an important arena, in terms of the way workers have pursued a range of grievances and cases in employment tribunals (Kirk, 2018). It is noticeable that as governments attempted to de-collectivize, there was a steady individualizing of rights – albeit without building the collective frameworks around which these rights could be easily enacted by workers and trade unions (Howell, 2005; Mustchin and Martínez Lucio, 2020). However, the state's 'withdrawal' is much more uneven, and it has had to supplement this strategy with projects aimed at transferring the responsibility of representation and conciliation to more indirect means of intervention through communication and 'conciliation' strategies and 'advice', along with a range of 'toolkits' and 'management standards' (Howell, 2005; Mustchin and Martínez Lucio, 2020).

Finally, the role of the state has increasingly been discussed in terms of its more coercive and concealed qualities, as noted earlier with respect to the 'Shrewsbury 24'. The debate on 'blacklisting' has been rethinking the way the state and employers have mobilized against the labour movement and rights-based organizations in the UK (Smith and Chamberlain, 2015). This underside of industrial relations has been a part of the general acceleration of anti-union politics (Dundon and Gall, 2013). The focus on attempts to undermine collective voice by employers has been paralleled with an interest in historical approaches to the role of right-wing think tanks and ideas, which have been steadily dissected as a persistent feature of the challenge to worker rights (Mustchin, 2019). Journals like *Historical Studies in Industrial Relations*, *Labor History* and *Labour History Review* have managed to develop and locate these challenges in relation to the deeper contours of British industrial relations historically. The remaking of the coercive and covert dimensions of the state has led to a growing interest in linking the discipline of industrial relations with criminology and law, that is, the concern with the ongoing attack on trade union rights (Bogg, 2016) and the ever-decreasing impact of deterrence against dangerous or illegal employment practices (Tombs and Whyte, 2013). Yet, running parallel with these developments, there has been a curious interest in whistleblowing as some form of palliative to the increasingly unregulated aspects of work and organizational activities (Lewis et al, 2015).

All these thematic developments and streams of academic intervention – and there are others – represent attempts to capture the contradictory nature of the state. The road to a 'neoliberal' context is not unilinear or predetermined, as the balance of forces in the nature of work and employment generate a series of pressures and counter-pressures to which the state has had to respond. In more general terms, the Keynesian welfare state and previous forms of 'collective' regulation have been severely undermined, but this has left a range of gaps and tensions, both societal and within organizations, which require some form of state response. To some extent, this has engendered an interest in regulation theory as a way of understanding the politics of fragmentation and the way the state intervenes (especially the work of Jessop [1990, 1995]). The increasingly financialized state also requires a range of interventions to ensure the reproduction of the workforce and some form of 'consensual' ideological dimension. The work of Howell (2005) has been key to placing these features in a historical context and in drawing attention to the manner in which the state reframes industrial relations – or, at least, attempts to do so. Hence, there has been an increasing level of interest in the state conceptually and some interventions with respect to the UK within industrial relations (Clark, 2000; Hyman, 2008; Martínez Lucio and MacKenzie, 2017).

Parallel with the development of these approaches has been the attempt to add a greater level of detail and depth to the concept of regulatory space by locating it in a broader discussion on the politics of regulation (Hancher and Moran, 1989; MacKenzie and Martínez Lucio, 2005, 2019; Inversi et al, 2017). These approaches have tried to broaden our view of the different actors of regulation (Heery and Frege, 2006; Bellemare et al, 2018). Of key concern is the way the state 'shares' or 'moves' its regulatory functions, and how political competition and tensions exists in terms of how these roles are allocated and controlled. That said, within industrial relations, regulation in terms of its levels, degrees of formality and contested spaces and roles has been a long-standing academic concern and, to some extent, marks the nature of the discipline. The work of Crouch (1993: 52–5) remains important for understanding the need to map the nature of industrial relations exchanges across a broader range of actors and, indeed, exchanges, even when the balance may be tilted in favour of some over others. An interdependence develops between actors; therefore, strong trade union movements are crucial to strong systems of industrial relations (Crouch, 1993). However, what we have seen is a range of other actors encroach into the space of regulation, such as consultancies, non-government organizations and others, and this has become part of the way regulation is increasingly understood. In the context of the decline of key institutional features, the industrial relations discipline has continued to widen its conception of regulation.

The failing 'stretched state'

The political projects attempting to socialize the neoliberal state during the Labour governments of the late 1990s and early 2000s were unable to sustain themselves in the context of financial crisis. More broadly, there is a view that the neoliberal turn and the ongoing embedding of the logics of privatization and managerialism within both economy and society have become an increasing reality, even in those states seen to herald an alternative approach to that of the UK (Baccaro and Howell, 2017). There seems to be a further push towards a greater degree of outsourcing and fragmentation within the state itself, as well as an embedding of the obsession with markets that it does not seem possible to dislodge (Davies, 2016).

The post-2008 period saw the brief counterpoints of the late 1990s and early 2000s superseded by a reassertion of attempts to limit the capacity of the state and its remit – something not unique to the UK (Heyes et al, 2012). The ongoing austerity measures imposed by government policy have had a negative social effect but seem to have generated the longer-term basis for greater social and industrial conflict (for discussions of the impact of austerity, see Grimshaw and Rubery, 2012; Williams and Scott, 2016), Increasingly, this shift in government policy has been tied to a new populist project that counters not only collectivism, as it did under Thatcherism, but also the relatively progressive and equality-related projects that had emerged in terms of individual rights. The types of developments that occurred in the 1980s and 1990s around marketization and social welfare changes have been intensified with an even greater role within the state for private capital in aspects of delivery and design. This has created a body of debate about the capabilities and limits of the state. Even proximity to the European Union prior to the decision to leave following the 2016 referendum did not lead to any cohesive or coherent moves towards a social state, and the uncertainty since Brexit has generated further fragmentation and unstable developments (for a discussion, see Teague and Donaghey, 2018). The COVID-19 crisis brought to light the impact of the state's underfunding and fragmentation during previous decades, which have generated increasing levels of inequality (see Nunn, 2016; James, 2021).

We are seeing greater interest in not only competition within regulatory spaces or the counterpointing of social and economic functions of the state – views that still see political possibilities or contradictions in the way the state intervenes – but also in the way the legacy of previous policy decisions, changes and economic developments have undermined the sustainability and effectiveness of the state. For many, the pandemic shed light on the way in which the political reform had undermined not only the social and economic infrastructure of the UK but also the very presence of the state and its abilities to engage and respond. The question of the state's relative autonomy (as Poulantzas [1973] put it; see also Miliband [1973]) has been the subject of much debate within the industrial relations tradition, notably, in terms of the de facto decline of that autonomy. However, much effort remains to be made in trying to map the continuing ways in which the local state and the devolved governments in Northern Ireland, Scotland and Wales have attempted to pick up the repeatedly dropped regulatory baton.

Conclusion

It is clear that interest in the state has not declined as a consequence of the ostensive retreat of the state but rather grown in reflection of the proliferation of forms of state roles. In turn, this reflects a broadening of interests within the field, building on and moving beyond the earlier focus of institutional industrial relations on trade unions and collective bargaining to become a more diverse field. This diversification has allowed for a greater sensitivity to the seismic yet contradictory shifts in the role of the state.

While the state enhances a more individualized orientation within industrial relations (Howell, 2005) and removes a range of social protections, it is also forced to constantly re-intervene into work- and employment-related issues to deal with the contradictory outcomes of such strategies (for a discussion of this irony, see Rubery, 2011). What is more, the state is expanding its role at the very time that it quantitatively limits its capacity and pushes the onus of regulation onto a wider set of, albeit under-resourced, public and private actors.

The field of industrial relations in the UK has been innovative and engaging in the way it maps this increasing 'stretched' and 'uneven' state, as we have partially outlined earlier. The presence of a series of contradictions and uneven roles within the state suggests that the analytical move to unpack the neoliberal state has allowed us to realize the broader consequences of change. The drawn-out crisis of the state in the UK and its increasingly porous qualities (something the current Conservative government intends to accelerate formally) have led to a patchwork of state institutions and roles that adopt different state projects in an uncoordinated manner. The problem is not solely one of a 'strong state' obsessed with 'markets' but, rather, one of a weak and fractured state obsessed with minimalist benchmarks and the problem of its public legitimacy at a time when the demand for social and employment rights has not dissipated. The story is not one of simply charting the road to neoliberalism but, rather, one of highlighting how the state becomes hamstrung by the very projects of reform, which has led to a need to rethink the way we view regulation and rights.

Acknowledgements

The authors wish to thank the editors and reviewers for their helpful comments on previous versions of this chapter.

References

Ackers, P. (2007) 'Collective bargaining as industrial democracy: Hugh Clegg and the political foundations of British industrial relations pluralism', *British Journal of Industrial Relations*, 45(1): 77–101.

Baccaro, L. and Howell, C. (2017) *Trajectories of Neoliberal Transformation: European Industrial Relations since the 1970s*, Cambridge: Cambridge University Press.

Bach, S. (2002) 'Public-sector employment relations reform under labour: muddling through on modernization?', *British Journal of Industrial Relations*, 40(2): 319–39.

Bellemare, G., Briand, L., Havard, C. and Naschberger, C. (2018) 'Users/patients as industrial relations actors: a structurationist analysis', *Relations industrielles/Industrial Relations*, 73(3): 486–516.

Beynon, H. (ed) (1985) *Digging Deeper: Issues in the Miners' Strike*, London: Verso.

Bogg, A. (2016) 'Beyond neo-liberalism: the Trade Union Act 2016 and the authoritarian state', *Industrial Law Journal*, 45(3): 299–336.

Byrne, D. (2018) 'The problem that is Labour local government', *Soundings*, 69: 50–61.

Clark, I. (1996) 'The state and the new industrial relations', in I.J. Beardwell (ed) *Contemporary Industrial Relations*, Oxford: Oxford University Press, pp 37–65.

Clark, I. (2000) *Governance, the State, Regulation and Industrial Relations*, London: Routledge.

Clegg, H.A. (1976) *Trade Unionism under Collective Bargaining*, Oxford: Blackwell.

Crouch, C. (1993) *Industrial Relations and European State Traditions*, Oxford: Oxford University Press.

Darlington, R. and Lyddon, D. (2001) *Glorious Summer: Class Struggle in Britain, 1972*, London: Bookmarks.

Davies, W. (2016) 'The new neoliberalism', *New Left Review*, 101: 121–34.

Dorey, P. (2019) *Comrades in Conflict: Labour, the Trade Unions and 1969's In Place of Strife*, Manchester: Manchester University Press.

Dundon, T. and Gall, G. (2013) 'Anti-unionism: contextual and thematic issues', in T. Dundon and G. Gall (eds) *Global Anti-unionism*, London: Palgrave Macmillan, pp 1–17.

Gamble, A. (1988) *The Free Economy and the Strong State: The Politics of Thatcherism*, London: Macmillan.

Garrahan, P. and Stewart, P. (1992) *The Nissan Enigma*, London: Mansell.

Grimshaw, D. and Rubery, J. (2012) 'The end of the UK's liberal collectivist social model? The implications of the Coalition government's policy during the austerity crisis', *Cambridge Journal of Economics*, 36(1): 105–26.

Grimshaw, D., Johnson, M., Marino, S. and Rubery, J. (2017) 'Towards more disorganised decentralization? Collective bargaining in the public sector under pay restraint', *Industrial Relations Journal*, 48(1): 22–41.

Grugulis, I. (2006) *Skills, Training and Human Resource Development: A Critical Text*, London: Macmillan.

Hall, S. (1988) *The Hard Road to Renewal*, London: Verso.

Hancher, L. and Moran, M. (1989) 'Organising regulatory space', in L. Hancher and M. Moran (eds) *Capitalism, Culture and Economic Regulation*, Oxford: Oxford University Press, pp 271–99.

Heery, E. and Frege, C. (2006) 'New actors in industrial relations', *British Journal of Industrial Relations*, 44(4): 601–4.

Heyes, J., Lewis, P. and Clark, I. (2012) 'Varieties of capitalism, neoliberalism and the economic crisis of 2008?', *Industrial Relations Journal*, 43(3): 222–41.

Howell, C. (2005) *Trade Unions and the State*, Princeton, NJ: Princeton University Press.

Hyman, R. (1975) *Industrial Relation: A Marxist Introduction*, London: MacMillan.

Hyman, R. (2008) 'The state in industrial relations', in P. Blyton, N. Bacon, J. Fiorito and E. Heery (eds) *The Sage Handbook of Industrial Relations*, London: Sage Publications, pp 258–83.

Hyman, R. and Brough, I. (1975) *Social Values and Industrial Relations: A Study of Fairness and Equality*, London: Blackwell.

Inversi, C., Buckley, L.A. and Dundon, T. (2017) 'An analytical framework for employment regulation: investigating the regulatory space', *Employee Relations*, 39(3): 291–307.

James, P. (ed) (2021) *HSE and Covid at Work: A Case of Regulatory Failure*, Liverpool: Institute of Employment Rights.

Jessop, B. (1990) *State Theory*, Oxford: Polity.

Jessop, B. (1995) 'The regulation approach, governance and post-Fordism: alternative perspectives on economic and political change?', *Economy and Society*, 24(3): 307–33.

Johnson, M. (2017) 'Implementing the living wage in UK local government', *Employee Relations*, 39(6): 840–9.

Kirk, E. (2018) 'The (re)organisation of conflict at work: mobilisation, counter-mobilisation and the displacement of grievance expressions', *Economic and Industrial Democracy*, 39(4): 639–60.

Lewis, D., D'Angelo, A. and Clarke, L. (2015) 'Industrial relations and the management of whistleblowing after the Francis Report: what can be learned from the evidence?', *Industrial Relations Journal*, 46(4): 312–27.

MacKenzie, R. and Martínez Lucio, M. (2005) 'The realities of regulatory change: beyond the fetish of deregulation', *Sociology*, 39(3): 499–517.

MacKenzie, R. and Martínez Lucio, M. (2014) 'The colonisation of employment regulation and industrial relations: dynamics and developments over five decades of change', *Labor History*, 55(2): 189–207.

MacKenzie, R. and Martínez Lucio, M. (2019) 'Regulation, migration and the implications for industrial relations', *Journal of Industrial Relations*, 61(2): 176–97.

Martínez Lucio, M. and MacKenzie, R. (2017) 'The state and the regulation of work and employment: theoretical contributions, forgotten lessons and new forms of engagement', *The International Journal of Human Resource Management*, 28(21): 2983–3002.

Martínez Lucio, M. and Stuart, M. (2011) 'The state, public policy and the renewal of HRM', *The International Journal of Human Resource Management*, 22(18): 3661–71.

McIlroy, J. and Croucher, R. (2013) 'British trade unions and the academics: the case of Unionlearn', *Capital & Class*, 37(2): 263–84.

Miliband, R. (1970) 'The capitalist state: reply to Nicos Poulantzas', *New Left Review*, 59(1): 53–60.

Miliband, R. (1973) 'Poulantzas and the capitalist state', *New Left Review*, 82(1): 83–93.

Mustchin, S. (2019) 'Right-wing pressure groups and the anti-union "movement" in Britain: aims of industry, neoliberalism, and industrial relations reform, 1942–1997', *Historical Studies in Industrial Relations*, 40: 69–101.

Mustchin, S. and Martínez Lucio, M. (2020) 'The evolving nature of labour inspection, enforcement of employment rights and the regulatory reach of the state in Britain', *Journal of Industrial Relations*, 62(5): 735–57.

Nunn, A. (2016) 'The production and reproduction of inequality in the UK in times of austerity', *British Politics*, 11(4): 469–87.

Panitch, L. (1981) 'Trade unions and the capitalist state', *New Left Review*, 125: 21–45.

Poulantzas, N. (1973) *Classes in Contemporary Capitalism*, London: NLB.

Rainbird, H. and Stuart, M. (2011) 'The state and the union learning agenda in England', *Work, Employment and Society*, 23(2): 202–17.

Rubery, J. (2011) 'Reconstruction amid deconstruction: or why we need more of the social in European social models', *Work, Employment and Society*, 25(4): 658–74.

Smith, D. and Chamberlain, P. (2015) *Blacklisted: The Secret War between Big Business and Union Activists*, London: New Internationalist.

Stuart, M. (2007) 'Introduction: the industrial relations of learning and training: a new consensus or a new politics?', *European Journal of Industrial Relations*, 13(3): 269–80.

Teague, P. and Donaghey, J. (2018) 'Brexit: EU social policy and the UK employment model', *Industrial Relations Journal*, 49(5–6): 512–33.

Tombs, S. and Whyte, D. (2013) 'The myths and realities of deterrence in workplace safety regulation', *British Journal of Criminology*, 53(5): 746–63.

Turnbull, E. (2022) *A Very British Conspiracy: The Shrewsbury 24 and the Campaign for Justice*, London: Verso Books.

Williams, S. and Scott, P. (eds) (2016) *Employment Relations under Coalition Government: The UK Experience, 2010–2015*, London: Routledge.

Winchester, D. (1983) 'Industrial relations in the public sector', in G. Bain (ed) *Industrial Relations in Britain*, Oxford: Blackwell, pp 155–78.

Yates, E. and Clark, I. (2018) 'The strategic economic governance of Greater Manchester's local labour market by the local state: implications for young workers', *Economic and Industrial Democracy*, 42(1): 27–49.

8

Labour Markets

Jill Rubery

Introduction

This chapter identifies the key changes that have been taking place in the labour market and how these are affecting people's experience of work and employment. Employment relations as a subject takes a different perspective on labour (Rubery, 2005, 2015) than that found in a standard economics text. Instead of focusing on the market and the aggregate demand and supply of different categories of labour, employment relations recognizes that most people are in jobs and not seeking to enter or change employment at any one point in time. Employment relationships thus depend on the characteristics of the organizations that are employing the workforce, the factors that lead to people entering the labour force and seeking employment, and the factors shaping their terms and conditions. Key recent trends on both demand and supply sides have led to significant change in these three dimensions: employing organizations have been transformed by the trends of financialization and fragmentation, seeking financial returns and lower costs and responsibilities through outsourcing; and the labour supply has been transformed by its increasing feminization. The key word to describe changes in the conditions of employment is 'flexibilization', reflecting not only changes in employer orientations and practices, as well as changes in the labour supply, but also changing employment regulations, uses of employment contracts and welfare state practices. This analysis of the labour market pre-dates the COVID-19 pandemic in two senses: not only were the trends visible long before COVID-19 but the first draft of the chapter was also completed before COVID-19. The main text is thus complemented by an extended conclusion that both explores the implications of COVID-19 and, indeed, the subsequent cost-of-living crisis for these longer-term trends, and considers the likely direction and force of future trends without a reversal of current policy agendas.

The changing nature of employing organizations

Four key trends have been reshaping the demand side of the labour market: the sectoral shift towards service activities; the increasingly global organization of both manufacturing and service operations (Gereffi, 2012); the fragmentation of employing organizations through the use of outsourcing (Marchington et al, 2005; Weil, 2017); and the financialization of companies, which is reorienting their key objectives and behaviour (Froud et al, 2006; Appelbaum and Batt, 2014).

While the move towards services is a worldwide phenomenon, the UK has been a leader of the pack in this respect, with the share of services in gross domestic product (GDP) (at 71 per cent) outstripping that in all European Union (EU) countries bar the tiny countries of Luxembourg and Malta.[1] When it comes to engagement in global production networks, for example, measured in relation to UK exports, the UK has a relatively low involvement, largely because of the importance of services in the UK's exports, which are mainly domestically produced (Ijtsma et al, 2018). The UK was particularly engaged in offshoring of call-centre activity, but as technologies have changed, this type of activity has either declined or, in some cases, been reshored.

Fragmentation through outsourcing within the UK has, however, continued to grow. This is particularly an issue in outsourcing by the public sector, which now accounts for about a third of public sector expenditure and has helped to spawn the growth of very large service companies despite their often poor performance record.[2] One of the largest – Carillion – collapsed in 2018, revealing what has been described as a major Ponzi scheme,[3] where growth was based on bidding for contracts that were inherently unprofitable while paying large sums to directors and raiding the pension fund.[4] While some outsourcing has always occurred and some areas have seen improvements in efficiency (for example, waste management, cleaning, catering and maintenance services [Institute for Government, 2019]), the spread of outsourcing to wider areas is breaking down competencies and specialist knowledge within the public sector.

Areas like probation services, fitness-to-work assessments, prisons and security services for the Olympics, to name but a few, have all been outsourced and have all been subject to major and publicized failures (Institute for Government, 2019). In large part, these are linked to the lack of appropriate knowledge and expertise, but outsourcing still continues, rising to a new high in the COVID-19 pandemic, as we discuss further later.

This move away from competition based on quality has been fuelled by the wider financialization of the economy. This term, though widely used, has many meanings, including simply the increasing dominance of the finance sector and the growth in financial transactions based on a proliferation of financial products relative to GDP. For some, it marks a new era or phase of capitalism; what it means for the labour market is not only the risk of debt-fuelled bubbles and the subsequent collapse of demand, as occurred in 2008, but also that individual companies and their often short-term owners (such as private equity funds [see Appelbaum and Batt, 2014]) are primarily concerned with financial returns on assets, however they are achieved, and not with the longer-term development of product or service advantage based on expertise or reputation. This is revealed in the examples of companies raiding pension funds and inflating directors' earnings before selling out or collapsing. However, it is also found in the car industry's reliance on the financing of car purchases for their profits rather than the making of the cars themselves (do Carmo et al, 2019) or in the asset stripping of the property owned by care-home providers (Hutton, 2020), leaving them vulnerable to collapse due to expensive rents on their properties.

These tendencies are reducing the focus of capital on the employment relationship as the basis for their activity. Companies' reliance on labour and labour's skills for the quality production of goods and services provided a key bargaining basis on which to build decent work agendas. However, the increasing focus on short-term gains, often through the exploitation of physical or financial assets, has reduced the apparent importance of the employment relationship for companies in meeting their profit objectives. As Boyer (2000: 112) notes, in countries like the US and the UK, 'the financial regime plays the central role that used to be attributed to the wage-labour nexus under Fordism'.

A final trend is the growth of the gig economy, though still only accounting for a minority of economic activity. In many respects, this phenomenon can be considered part of both fragmentation and financialization (ILO, 2021). Platform work is based on outsourcing, though requiring a much more detailed unbundling of tasks provided via algorithms than is the case with the outsourcing of whole activities to subcontractors. In both cases, the outcome is to create a distance or disconnect between those performing work tasks and those demanding and using the tasks. The growth of the gig economy has also been facilitated by the disconnect under financialization between the viability of the real economy business model and economic survival, for example, Uber has yet to record a positive profit but continues to receive large investments from venture capitalists (ILO, 2021). While Uber is associated with poor employment practices, it may ultimately be more interested in displacing the employment relationship as its key means of functioning through the development of driverless cars than in reconstructing the employment relationship.

Despite these processes of disassociation of capital from the management of the employment relationship, most workers are still in the direct employment of an employer, even if, as we discuss later, the relationship is hollowed out and the direct employer is acting as a subcontractor for the main client. Moreover, far from evidence of the widespread displacement of labour, employment rates in the UK economy pre-COVID-19 were at a record high. As debates take off on the end of work (Srnicek and Williams, 2015; Susskind, 2020), we also find a tendency for more and more people to be drawn into the labour market, as we discuss next.

The changing labour supply

The most sustained and significant change in the composition of the labour supply in the UK – and all advanced countries – has been the steady increase in the participation of women. This feminization of the employment system has not resulted in gender equality; rather, women still do the lion's share of unpaid work and, consequently, in the UK, tend to work part-time and are unable to provide the long hours of work expected in high-level jobs in the period of peak childcare responsibilities. Nevertheless, women now constitute around 48 per cent of all in employment and over 38 per cent of all full-time workers.[5] Women no longer normally interrupt their employment participation at childbirth but, instead, remain in employment, aided by rights to maternity leave. However, discrimination, including the dismissal of women during pregnancy and maternity leave, is common (EHRC and BIS, 2016). The factors generating women's increased labour supply are multiple. In the initial phase, it can be argued to have been the demand for female labour in the growing services sectors that drove the increased participation. However, the outcome has been a permanent attachment to the labour market, sustained by adjustments of household budgets and consumption patterns to two earners, by the declining availability of family wages for men and, more importantly, by changes in the aspiration and expectations of women themselves, fuelled by their increasing investments in education, which outstrip those of men (Rubery and Rafferty, 2013).

A second significant trend has, in fact, been towards a much higher share of labour market participants with higher education, with over half of 25- to 34-year-olds now having tertiary education compared to around two fifths of those aged 55 to 64 in the UK (OECD, 2020). There is much dispute as to whether there has been a similar rise in the demand for skilled labour, for as a higher share of a cohort enters higher education, so employers tend to raise their demands for new starters to have higher qualifications, even without any significant change in the job content. Overall, the evidence is mixed: higher-skilled jobs have expanded, though not enough to absorb all the increases in the higher educated. The result has been a rising trend in overeducation for both men and women since 2010, such that one in six workers are estimated to be overeducated for their current job in 2017 (ONS, 2019). This rise in higher education is argued by Keep (2020) to be the consequence of the lack of training provided by employers in the UK, resulting in increased reliance on higher education as the default policy option.

One of the consequences of the extension of higher education is that a high share of young people have been taken out of the labour market, except for casual employment to support their studies. This growth in a 'casual' youth labour force has probably contributed to the increasing complexity and uncertainty experienced in making transitions to more secure employment for the school leavers who do not go on to further training, particularly for those from more socially disadvantaged backgrounds (Sanderson, 2020). At the other end of the age spectrum, there has been a rapid increase in the employment rates of older workers. In large part, this is due to the raising of the state pension age, particularly for women, and reduced opportunities in occupational pension schemes for early retirement.[6] However, it also reflects the change in women's work behaviour over recent decades; now, most women moving into the older age categories did not end their labour market participation even when their children were small and are thus more likely to also stay in work as their children grow up.

Finally, but by no means least, there has been a large growth in migration, particularly from the EU, though also due to waves of non-EU migration linked to both economic and political factors. The increase in the post-2004 period in EU migration[7] can be attributed, in part, to the UK being one of only three EU countries not to impose restrictions on migration from new member states, but it has been further fuelled by the relatively strong demand for labour in the UK after the financial crisis, certainly compared with the Southern European countries, as well as Eastern European member states.

Changing policy and regulatory systems

The labour market is shaped not only by the characteristics and behaviours of the main protagonists – those who employ and those who work – but also by the institutional and social contexts in which they are operating. Employment relations scholars tend to focus on the core institutional arrangements shaping the employment relationship, such as union organization, collective bargaining and employment rights, but there is a strong case for widening this perspective to include, for example, the welfare and family system and training policies.

Although the major declines in coverage of collective bargaining and union organization occurred in the 1980s, recent years have witnessed a further narrowing of collective regulation. Furthermore, although collective regulation in the public sector still exists in principle, long-term restrictions on pay bargaining imposed under austerity policies have hollowed out even these remaining areas of collective regulation. In this context, legal regulation has taken on greater importance, though from a starting point of very limited regulation due to both the voluntarist tradition in UK employment relations and the adoption of a neoliberal approach by governments from the 1980s onwards. Moreover, this expansion of legal employment rights is largely due to European law rather than a UK-driven initiative; important European-driven rights include equal treatment for those on non-standard forms of employment, equality laws, working-time regulations and the protection of employment rights under outsourcing (TUC, 2011). Notable other changes in principle include: protections under public sector outsourcing that slowed it down in the 1980s by reducing cost advantages; the development of a wide range of protected characteristics under discrimination law that underpinned the Equalities Act 2010; the provision of mandatory paid holidays, which proved important for part-timers, who were often denied paid holidays in the past; the extension of maternity leave to all; and the principle of equal treatment for part-time and fixed-term contract workers, even if it has limited impact due to the concentration of part-time work in firms and sectors where full-timers also have poor employment conditions. However, what is more remarkable about the UK labour market is the lack of employment rights, particularly with respect to issues of protection against unfair dismissal and working time. Unfair-dismissal protection only applies after two years' continuous service, and there is a voluntary opt-out from maximum working hours, but there is also no protection against zero- or minimum-hours contracts and no restrictions on flexible scheduling (Grimshaw et al, 2016).

There are two main areas where the UK has gone a bit further than mandated by European law. The first is in relation to equality duties and gender-pay-gap reporting, though the practical impact of these measures on actual practice is questionable (Conley and Page, 2010; EHRC, 2019). Moreover, there has been a postponement of requirements to report on gender pay gaps under the COVID-19 pandemic, and new proposals for a European directive on pay-transparency measures will not apply to post-Brexit UK. The second area where new legal rights were not mandated by European law is the introduction of the National Minimum Wage. Most member states have either a national minimum wage or relatively comprehensive coverage of collectively agreed minimum wages, but it was only in 2022 that the Minimum Wage Directive was approved, which sets out measures to ensure that the level of the minimum wage is adequate.[8] Again, this directive will not apply to the UK, but even without any external mandate, the UK's National Minimum Wage has had a major impact on the UK's labour market and in shaping the wage structure, not only by raising the floor but also by compressing wages at the bottom end of the labour market, as we discuss later in identifying key labour market outcomes (Low Pay Commission, 2019).

The UK labour market is also shaped by its welfare state and taxation systems. The policy of exempting earnings up to a threshold from national insurance contributions by both employees and employers provides a basis for the high level of low-paid part-time work in the UK, reinforced by the lack of affordable childcare. It also leaves around 2 million people, 70 per cent of them women, ineligible for basic sick pay or unemployment benefits.[9] The development of some free childcare provision, including 30 hours per week for three-year-olds from 2015, has been beneficial, but there have been problems of supply, as the free childcare is funded at below-market costs, leading to a shortfall of private sector provision.[10] Another characteristic of the UK taxation system is the relatively low taxation of the self-employed. Coupled with the right to free healthcare, this enables the take-up of self-employment jobs in the gig economy and elsewhere without serious loss of social protection rights or the alternative of high rates of social security contributions, as applies to the self-employed in many European countries.

The growth of low-paid employment is also shaped by policies towards welfare benefits. The UK has long adopted a strong work-first policy, applying sanctions to those who do not search for or take up available jobs of whatever quality. The expansion of in-work tax credits from the end of the 1990s onwards has also normalized and legitimized low-paid work, even though only household heads receive the in-work benefits. The new policy of integrating in-work tax credits with unemployment benefits is potentially laying the foundations for a further increase in the intensity of the work-first policy, with Universal Credit recipients expected to accept whatever jobs are available, including zero-hours contracts (previously jobs had to guarantee 16 or 30 hours to move off unemployment benefits to tax credits), and requiring recipients to search for work for up to 35 hours (if paid at the minimum-wage level) while not requiring employers to provide contracts guaranteeing hours or fixed schedules of work (Millar and Bennett, 2017).

Labour market outcomes

The labour market in the UK is characterized by four key features that reflect the changing nature of employers, the labour force and the policy and regulatory context. The first development is the concentration of pay around the National Minimum Wage. The upward trend in the level of the National Minimum Wage, further accelerated by the 2016 introduction of a higher National Living Wage for those aged over 25 (from 2021 for those aged 22 and above) has led to recent growth in earnings for those at the bottom of the labour market. However, the impact has also been to turn the National Minimum Wage into the going rate for jobs for a wide segment of the labour market. While those earning close to the minimum wage may receive some increases in pay after a rise in the National Minimum Wage, it has tended to be less than the increase in the National Minimum Wage itself, thus leading to compressed pay in the bottom segment of the labour market (Low Pay Commission, 2019).

The second feature is the growth of job and income insecurity with the spread of zero- and minimum-hours contracts both inside and outside the gig economy. The Office for National Statistics (ONS) estimates that just short of a million workers, or around 3.0 per cent of those in employment, were on zero-hours contracts in December 2019,[11] but there are probably even more given a guarantee of a minimum number of hours but expected to work extra hours to meet employer needs (IDS, 2017). There is also evidence of increasing instability in earnings, especially for the lowest paid (Resolution Foundation, 2018). While some flexible working is driven by employee needs, especially when they take on care responsibilities, much of the flexibility is employer-driven flexible working, or 'one-sided flexibility' as, for example, the Low Pay Commission has termed it.

The third feature is a high level of wage inequality in the UK labour market, associated with the growth of individualized pay bargaining under management-determined pay systems. Even though the higher National Minimum Wage has reduced wage inequality in the bottom half of the distribution, the UK still has high overall wage inequality. The ratio of earnings for the top 10 per cent to the bottom 10 per cent of earnings is 3.42, with 22 out of 36 Organisation for Economic Co-operation and Development countries recording lower wage inequality in 2018, including all but two from the 'old' Europe (EU member states prior to 2004), namely, Portugal and Ireland. Inequality in the UK is still well below that in the US, where the top to bottom decile ratio stands at 4.95.[12] This high pay also often comes with a price: that of willingness to work wherever and whenever, with the associated long and variable working hours a barrier to access to higher-paying jobs for anyone with care responsibilities or non-work commitments. It is the highest paid that now work the longest hours, often involving unpaid overtime, while those in low-paid jobs are often underemployed and seeking more hours (Bangham, 2020), exacerbating income inequalities.

The fourth feature is the climate of fear induced by the sanctions-focused welfare system (Greer, 2016) and the lack of dignity for those unable to work or to find work. This hostile environment to those claiming benefits – as described by the special United Nations (UN) Rapporteur on Poverty Philip Alston – may, in part, account for the high growth of self-employment and the willingness of people to accept highly insecure and low-paid work:

The initial rationales for reform were to reduce overall expenditures and to promote employment as the principal 'cure' for poverty. But when large-scale poverty persisted despite a booming economy and very high levels of employment, the Government chose not to adjust course. Instead, it doubled down on a parallel agenda to reduce benefits by every means available, including constant reductions in benefit levels, ever-more-demanding conditions, harsher penalties, depersonalization, stigmatization, and virtually eliminating the option of using the legal system to vindicate rights. The basic message, delivered in the language of managerial efficiency and automation, is that almost any alternative will be more tolerable than seeking to obtain government benefits. (Alston, 2018: 20)

What this adds up to is a hollowing out of the notion of decent work for a high share of those in employment, exacerbated by both the decline in responsible, visible and good employers, and the degradation of both the process of claiming social support and the level of support available.

The UK employment system, the COVID-19 pandemic and its aftermath

One of the impacts of the COVID-19 pandemic was to reveal many of the key fault lines in the UK's employment system, as described earlier. The most obvious has been the meagre benefit levels, particularly statutory sick pay (SSP), which is the lowest among EU countries except for Malta. This has had the consequence of reducing ability to comply with the need to self-isolate, as workers often could not simply afford to self-isolate if they only receive SSP. These problems are further exacerbated by the exclusion of up to 2 million employees from even these rights. Tacit acknowledgement of the punitive level of benefits was indicated by the provision of £500 – over 2.5 times SSP – to those required to self-isolate (though with rights restricted to those claiming Universal Credit). Further acknowledgement of the excessively low benefits was implicit in the temporary uplift to the basic Universal Credit payment to bring them up to the already-meagre SSP benefit level. However, the main way in which the extremely low benefits of the unemployed were kept out of the spotlight has been through the furlough and the self-employed income support schemes. By setting these benefits at 80 per cent of wages and past profits, the government averted the revolt that would surely have come from millions of well-paid workers being expected to survive on well under £100 a week. This concern is perhaps indicated by the decision to stop the £20-a-week supplement once it appeared that most in normally secure employment would not need to have recourse to benefits and to reinstate the requirement for up to 35 hours of active job search for claimants.

The support system during COVID-19 carried many of the hallmarks of the UK's neoliberal labour market. All decisions were at the discretion of the employer, with no rights for workers – a particular problem for those claiming furlough on grounds of childcare and homeschooling in the pandemic. In contrast, in the EU16, countries provided parental leave as an employee right (Rubery and Tavora, 2021). The Trades Union Congress (TUC) found that seven out of ten mothers responding to a survey had been refused furlough on these grounds by their employer.[13] Other aspects of the UK system that have come to the fore include the high levels of inequalities in the labour market; these have been exacerbated under COVID-19, as the more disadvantaged have been less able to work from home and have thus faced more health risks and more risks of job and income loss, leading to rising debt levels (IFS, 2021). In comparison, the more educated and middle classes were able to increase their savings, in part, because they were more able to continue working due to the rapid roll-out of remote working. The normalization of working from home could assist some women to maintain their careers and involve more men in childcare; nevertheless, the outcome could be new forms of gender segregation, with women expected to mainly work from home while men return to the office. In relation to the self-employed and those on precarious contracts, the government may appear to have provided relatively inclusive support – for example, by allowing furlough on the basis of actual earnings, not on contracted hours - but the effectiveness of these inclusionary measures again depended on the actions of employers. Furthermore, when it came to freelancers, many were effectively excluded due to the use of short-term direct contracts, so that they were neither eligible for furlough or the self-employed support.

Beyond these effects on households and individuals, the UK labour market system has also been implicated in some of the major failings in the management of the COVID-19 pandemic. The high rate of death among care-home residents can, in part, be traced back to the use of agency workers, who transmitted COVID-19 between care homes, but agency workers were used because of the shortage of care staff, reflecting the low wages and zero-hours contracts endemic in this sector.[14] Further, although the government took major steps to fund activities to deal with the pandemic, their default position was to outsource these activities to private sector companies, often to ones with no expertise in the area, including the test-and-trace system, where £37 billion was allocated to the programme over two years but the effectiveness rated as lamentable.[15] In contrast, the much more successful vaccination programme was managed by the NHS itself.

However, these problems, which emerged during the pandemic and the early stages of recovery, soon gave way to another set of problems and concerns that again revealed fault lines in the UK's labour market system. First of all, many sectors started experiencing labour shortages, partly resulting from Brexit and the outflow of migrant labour but also because of a rise in inactivity among the UK resident workforce, particularly older people, possibly linked to increasing ill health due to COVID-19.[16] These shortages put some upward pressure on wages in the private sector, but there was little sign of government willingness to respond to the public mood during COVID-19, expressed through a nationwide clap, that there was a need to revalue the work performed by public service workers, whether directly employed by the government or employed by private sector organizations but funded by the state, such as social care workers. Public service workers may have been disappointed by the failure to make good some of the erosion of their wages during the long period of austerity in return for their efforts under COVID-19, but this disappointment turned to strike action[17] as energy prices soared and the cost-of-living crisis hit in frustration at the government's continued refusal to maintain the real value of their wages. This has sparked another 'winter of discontent' in 2022/23 as public service strikes became widespread, fuelled by much the same problems as in the 1978 Winter of Discontent, namely, assumptions by government that public sector workers should bear the cost of rising prices.

Conclusion

The trends identified pre-COVID-19 and the new problems emerging post-COVID-19, linked also to the impact of Brexit and the energy and cost-of-living crises, suggest the need to kickstart a major debate on what kind of labour market and employment system we want and need. The expected further growth of the gig economy and associated bogus self-employment, coupled with predicted job displacement from the next phase of technological development, can only add to the problems identified unless there is a change of course. This does not mean that we will see an end to the notion of a standard employment contract; not only do many employers still need the commitment of an established workforce but a stable society also requires that people have access to relatively stable incomes and jobs to enable them to plan their lives, form families and provide for their dependants. To a large extent, the importance of the maintenance of stable employment relationships for stable economies and societies explains the surprising interventions during COVID-19 by neoliberal-minded governments, such as that in the UK, to ensure that employment relationships were largely maintained rather than discontinued. However, in a context of rising inflation, continued low productivity growth and threats to employment rights, including rights to strike as one of the apparent Brexit benefits, conditions of work are likely to further deteriorate and segment. This prediction is despite the warm words on 'building back better' that pervaded the first phase of the COVID-19 pandemic. Any reversal of these trends is thus likely to be reliant on the election of a government committed to promoting decent work through legal and collective regulation, and to providing dignified support for the unemployed.

Notes

[1] See: https://data.worldbank.org/indicator/NV.SRV.TOTL.ZS
[2] See: www.instituteforgovernment.org.uk/sites/default/files/publications/IfG_procur ement_WEB_4.pdf
[3] See: www.ft.com/content/a4dd80be-f9f1-11e7-a492-2c9be7f3120a
[4] See: www.theguardian.com/money/2018/jan/16/after-carillion-how-many-firms-can-the-pensions-lifeboat-rescue
[5] See: www.nomisweb.co.uk/datasets/aps210/reports/employment-by-status-and-occupat ion?compare=K02000001
[6] ONS data show that the employment rates of 50- to 64-year-olds rose by 9 percentage points for men to 78 per cent during 2000–19 but by 15 percentage points for women to 68 per cent over the same period (see: https://www.gov.uk/government/collections/economic-labour-market-status-of-individuals-aged-50-and-over).
[7] See: https://migrationobservatory.ox.ac.uk/resources/briefings/eu-migrat ion-to-and-from-the-uk/
[8] See: www.euractiv.com/section/economy-jobs/news/eu-minimum-wage-directive-gets-final-stamp-of-approval/
[9] See: www.tuc.org.uk/news/1-10-women-dont-earn-enough-qualify-sick-pay-tuc-analy sis-reveals
[10] See: https://wbg.org.uk/wp-content/uploads/2017/11/childcare-pre-budget-nov-2017-final.pdf
[11] See: www.ons.gov.uk/employmentandlabourmarket/peopleinwork/employmentandem ployeetypes/datasets/emp17peopleinemploymentonzerohourscontracts/current
[12] See: https://stats.oecd.org/Index.aspx?DataSetCode=DEC_I#
[13] See: www.tuc.org.uk/news/tuc-poll-7-10-requests-furlough-turned-down-work ing-mums
[14] See: https://blog.ons.gov.uk/2020/07/03/coronavirus-in-care-homes-what-the-latest-ons-research-tells-us/
[15] See: https://committees.parliament.uk/publications/4976/documents/50058/default/
[16] See: www.ons.gov.uk/employmentandlabourmarket/peoplenotinwork/economicinactiv ity/articles/halfamillionmorepeopleareoutofthelabourforcebecauseoflongtermsickness/ 2022-11-10
[17] See: www.ft.com/content/ce5d7629-b7bf-46dd-bb7a-ff177f1f4ca5

References

Alston, P. (2018) 'Report of the Special Rapporteur on Extreme Poverty and Human Rights', UN Human Rights Council. Available at: https://digitallibrary.un.org/record/3806308?ln=en#record-files-collapse-header

Appelbaum, E. and Batt, R. (2014) *Private Equity at Work: When Wall Street Manages Main Street*, New York: Russell Sage Foundation.

Bangham, G. (2020) 'The times they aren't a-changin': why working hours have stopped falling in London and the UK', Resolution Foundation, January.

Boyer, R. (2000) 'Is a finance-led growth regime a viable alternative to Fordism? A Preliminary analysis', *Economy and Society*, 29(1): 111–45.

Conley, H. and Page, M. (2010) 'The gender equality duty in local government: the prospects for integration', *Industrial Law Journal*, 39(3): 321–5.

Do Carmo, M., Sacomano Neto, M. and Cesar Donadone, J. (2019) 'Financialization in the automotive industry: shareholders, managers, and salaries', *Journal of Economic Issues*, LIII(3): 841–62.

EHRC (Equality and Human Rights Commission) (2019) 'The gender pay gap – where are we now?'. Available at: www.equalityhumanrights.com/en/our-work/blogs/gender-pay-gap-%E2%80%93-where-are-we-now

EHRC and BIS (Department for Business, Innovation & Skills) (2016) 'Pregnancy and maternity-related discrimination and disadvantage: summary of findings'. Available at: www.gov.uk/government/publications/pregnancy-and-maternity-related-discrimination-and-disadvantage-final-reports

Froud, J., Johal, S., Leaver, A. and Williams, K. (2006) *Financialization and Strategy: Narrative and Numbers*, London: Routledge.

Gereffi, G. (2012) 'Why the world suddenly cares about global supply chains', *Journal of Supply Chain Management*, 48(3): 24–32.

Greer, I. (2016) 'Welfare reform, precarity and the re-commodification of labour', *Work, Employment and Society*, 30(1): 162–73.

Grimshaw, D., Johnson, M., Rubery, J. and Kaizer, A. (2016) 'Reducing precarious work: protective gaps and the role of social dialogue', European Work and Employment Research Centre, Manchester Business School. Available at: https://documents.manchester.ac.uk/display.aspx?DocID=48958

Hutton, W. (2020) 'First, private equity holds us to ransom. Now it wants us to bail out its losses', *The Observer*, 23 August.

IDS (Incomes Data Services) (2017) 'Minimum and zero hours contracts and low-paid staff', Low Pay Commission. Available at: https://assets.publishing.service.gov.uk/government/uploads/system/uploads/attachment_data/file/772558/Minimum_and_zero_hours_contracts_IDR_October_2018_FINAL.pdf

IFS (Institute for Fiscal Studies) (2021) *COVID-19 and Inequalities (IFS Deaton Review)*, London: IFS.

Ijtsma, P., Levell, P., Los, B. and Timmer, M.P. (2018) 'The UK's participation in global value chains and its implications for post-Brexit trade policy', *Fiscal Studies*, 39(4): 651–83.

ILO (International Labour Organisation) (2021) *The Role of Digital Labour Platforms in Transforming the World of Work*, Geneva: ILO.

Institute for Government (2019) 'Government outsourcing: what has worked and what needs reform?'. Available at: www.instituteforgovernment.org.uk/publications/government-outsourcing-reform

Keep, E. (2020) 'Employers, the ghost at the feast', *Journal of Education and Work*, 33(7–8): 500–6.

Low Pay Commission (2019) *Twenty Years of the National Minimum Wage*, London: Low Pay Commission. Available at: https://assets.publishing.serv ice.gov.uk/government/uploads/system/uploads/attachment_data/file/ 790910/20_years_of_the_National_Minimum_Wage_-_a_history_of_ the_UK_minimum_wage_and_its_effects.pdf

Marchington, M., Grimshaw, D., Rubery, J. and Willmott, H. (eds) (2005) *Fragmenting Work: Blurring Boundaries and Disordering Hierarchies*, Oxford: Oxford University Press.

Millar, J. and Bennett, F. (2017) 'Universal Credit: assumptions, contradictions and virtual reality', *Social Policy and Society*, 16(2): 169–82.

OECD (Organisation for Economic Co-operation and Development) (2020) *Education at a Glance*, Paris: OECD.

ONS (Office for National Statistics) (2019) 'Overeducation and hourly wages in the UK labour market: 2006 to 2017'. Available at: www.ons. gov.uk/economy/nationalaccounts/uksectoraccounts/compendium/eco nomicreview/april2019/overeducationandhourlywagesintheuklabourm arket2006to2017

Resolution Foundation (2018) 'Irregular payments: assessing the breadth and depth of month to month earnings volatility'. Available at: www.resol utionfoundation.org/publications/irregular-payments/

Rubery, J. (2005) 'Labour markets and flexibility', in S. Ackroyd, R. Batt, P. Thompson and P.S. Tolbert (ed) *The Oxford Handbook of Work and Organization*, Oxford: Oxford University Press, pp 31–51.

Rubery, J. (2015) 'Change at work: feminisation, flexibilisation, fragmentation and financialisation', *Employee Relations*, 37(6): 633–44.

Rubery, J. and Rafferty, A. (2013) 'Women and recession revisited', *Work, Employment and Society*, 27(3): 414–32.

Rubery, J. and Tavora, I. (2021) 'The Covid-19 crisis and gender equality', in B. Vanhercke, S. Spasova and B. Fronteddu (eds) *Social Policy in the EU*, Brussels: ETUI, pp 71–96. Available at: www.etui.org/sites/default/ files/2021-01/06-Chapter4-The%20Covid%E2%80%9119%20crisis%20 and%20gender%20equality.pdf

Sanderson, E. (2020) 'Youth transitions to employment: longitudinal evidence from marginalised young people in England', *Journal of Youth Studies*, 23(10): 1310–29.

Srnicek, N. and Williams, A. (2015) *Inventing the Future: Postcapitalism and a World Without Work*, London: Verso Books.

Susskind, D. (2020) *A World Without Work: Technology, Automation and How we Should Respond*, London, Penguin.

TUC (Trades Union Congress) (2016) *UK Employment Rights and the EU*, London: TUC.

Weil, D. (2017) *The Fissured Workplace*, Cambridge, MA: Harvard University Press.

9

Industrial Relations and Labour Law: Recovery of a Shared Tradition?

Ruth Dukes and Eleanor Kirk

Introduction

In the UK, the scholarly disciplines of industrial relations (IR) and labour law have common roots, above all, in the pioneering work of Sidney and Beatrice Webb. Since the 1980s, the field, or fields, of study have been transformed, in part, by complex and partially intertwined processes of 'juridification' and human resource (HR) managerialization. Notwithstanding the shared heritage of labour law and IR, deepening disciplinary silos have meant that these processes have been studied, for the most part, in isolation from one another. Today, the 'fissuring' and precarization of work suggests the need for a sociology, or economic sociology, of labour law that would bring together empirical study and normative legal reasoning to identify the kind of law that might help to create more secure and equitable working relations in a wide variety of work settings.

Intertwined roots, forking branches

Sidney and Beatrice Webb are often cited as the founders of the field of IR (Kaufman, 2014). As part of IR's 'pre-history' (Voskiterian, 2010: 9), the Webbs provided a detailed account of the emergence and development of trade unionism, in which they identified a very significant role in the struggle for working-class emancipation for the 'method of legal enactment' – in combination with the methods of mutual insurance and collective bargaining (Webb and Webb, 1897). They also proposed a sophisticated understanding of collective bargaining as creating a kind of 'Magna Carta' for industry, performing an analogous function to political constitutions, namely, limiting the otherwise absolute power of the sovereign, or employer, and establishing democratic decision-making procedures instead. From the Webbs, scholars of IR and labour law alike inherited a shared conception of IR institutions, including law, as 'context specific', changing over time and assuming different forms in different locations (Flanders and Clegg, 1954a). Institutions were understood to be shaped, above all, by class conflict and power disparities, and by other features of the wider political economy. The dominant tradition in IR, as represented by the Oxford School, was oriented towards policy making and placed particular emphasis on the discovery of practically useful knowledge through the application of empirical and comparative methods, in preference to abstract, grand theory (Ackers and Wilkinson, 2005).

Credit for the founding of the discipline of labour law in the UK is usually accorded to Otto Kahn-Freund, a German–Jewish scholar and practising lawyer who escaped the Nazis in 1933 and settled for the remainder of his life in England. In Germany, he had studied labour law under Hugo Sinzheimer, whose scholarship was deeply influenced by the Webbs, or at least by a conviction similar to theirs that labour law and collective bargaining performed, above all, a democratizing function (Dukes, 2014). Just as Sinzheimer had done, Kahn-Freund based his very definition of labour law as a distinct legal discipline upon a sociologically informed understanding of the nature of the employment relationship and the social condition of the worker. Labour law was necessary, so the argument went, because private law was not up to the task of regulating working relations. The worker had no freedom of contract because he was subordinated to the employer; a collective agreement was not a contract between the union and the employer's organization but a kind of statute, or constitution, which laid down rules that were to apply across whole workplaces, companies or sectors. Seeking, in the 1950s and 1960s, to construct an empirically informed understanding of employment relations that was specific to practices in the UK, he turned to colleagues working in the field of IR and especially the Oxford School. In 1954, he contributed a chapter on the 'Legal framework' to Flanders and Clegg's (1954b) *System of Industrial Relations in Great Britain*. Emphasizing the benefits of the British 'voluntary system' and characterizing the relevant statutory rules as primarily a prop to voluntary collective bargaining, the chapter was strikingly similar in several respects to a text published by Flanders two years previously (Flanders, 1952; see also Kahn-Freund, 1954). In the 1960s, Kahn-Freund worked together with Flanders, Clegg and McCarthy in his role as a member of the Donovan Commission (Clegg, 1983). He was also an active member of the British Universities Industrial Relations Association (BUIRA), attending conferences and annual general meetings (Voskeritsian, 2010: 15), and a member of, and sometime speaker at, the Manchester Industrial Relations Society (Darlington, 2004).

During the course of the 1960s and 1970s, the collaboration between Kahn-Freund and the Oxford School extended beyond those particular individuals to encompass a whole generation of labour law scholars and 'industrial relations scholars with a legal bent', chief among them Bill Wedderburn, Paul O'Higgins, Roy Lewis, Jon Clark and Bob Hepple (Davies and Freedland, 2002: 769). The dominant tradition in labour law scholarship became and remained, broadly speaking, socio-legal in nature, aimed at understanding the 'law in context' and at assessing whether particular legal provisions had achieved the policy aims that had motivated their adoption or, alternatively, had had any unintended consequences (Simpson, 2001). In part, perhaps, because of their accommodation in law departments and the adaptation of their research to specialist law journals and disciplinary conventions, most labour law academics did not again enjoy the degree of close contact and collaboration with IR colleagues that Kahn-Freund had done. For their part, IR scholars' continued adherence to the principle of voluntarism and their preoccupation with productivity bargaining and with internal conflicts of interest between union leaders and the shop floor meant little detailed engagement with questions of law (Kaufman, 2014: 17). Those who engaged in comparative IR scholarship developed an early form of comparative institutionalism, though not one that was much concerned with legal institutions (Crouch and Pizzorno, 1978).

The changing nature of IR and labour law

From the 1980s, deindustrialization and the weakening and sidelining of trade unions and collective bargaining transformed the field of study of IR (Waddington et al, 2019). In labour law too, as outlined later, a set of very significant changes occurred, reflecting or even hastening the progressive demise of collective institutions. Together, these changes may be thought of in terms of a process or processes of 'juridification' (Clark and Wedderburn, 1987; Heery, 2010); however, the term is misleading if it is understood to suggest that a field once characterized by state abstentionism and an 'absence' of law became increasingly tightly legally regulated, that is, that collectively agreed rules were simply replaced by legal rules conferring rights and obligations upon individuals (Bogg, 2019). An indisputable increase in the volume of labour law, or employment law, across the decades occurred for a complex set of reasons, with complicated results (Taylor and Emir, 2006).[1] When employment rights were first introduced in the 1960s and early 1970s, for example, the understanding was that these would supplement and support, rather than replace, collective bargaining. Statutory rights would create a 'floor', as Lord Wedderburn famously put it, upon which collective bargaining could then build (Wedderburn, 1971: 39). Counterintuitively, the deregulatory policies of the Thatcher-led government of the 1980s also resulted in more, rather than less, law, as a cursory comparison of the trade union legislation of 1979 with that of 1997 demonstrates. Legislating in furtherance of the aims of weakening or restricting the scope of application of existing worker-protective measures, of limiting the collective rights and freedoms of workers, and of imposing greater legal controls on internal trade union democracy resulted overwhelmingly in the complication, rather than simplification, of existing legal provisions (Davies and Freedland, 1993: 425–61).

Under New Labour, the statutory rights of individual workers were expanded through the introduction of the National Minimum Wage, working-time regulations and a suite of 'family-friendly' provisions, and the extension of equality law to cover additional 'protected characteristics' (Davies and Freedland, 2007). The Human Rights Act 1998 and UK accession to the Social Chapter of the Maastricht Treaty combined to add an additional layer of human rights and fundamental (European) rights to the field of employment relations, extending law's reach – or the perception of law's reach – yet further. Disappointed perhaps by New Labour's refusal to reverse the egregiously anti-union measures of previous administrations, scholars of labour law turned increasingly to the judiciary as a potential force for good when it came to the furtherance of workers' interests, seen as a potential brake on the deregulatory impulses that could no longer be attributed solely to the Conservative Party. It became common practice in labour law to analyse the extent of the constraints posed by human rights on the freedom of action of the legislature and the development of the common law, or to refer to human rights as providing grounds for an expansive reading of worker protective statutory provisions. The aim here was not only to assist the courts or potential litigants but also, in some cases, to strengthen political arguments for legislative change or – where deregulation was threatened – more modestly for the maintenance of the status quo. In an era in which the language of 'industrial democracy' and 'industrial citizenship' had lost its currency, even those scholars who remained more sceptical about the likely success of such 'human rights strategizing' turned readily to human rights and international labour law to provide a justification for the normative thrust of their legal analysis (Ewing, 2010). In the field of labour law, as elsewhere, human rights had become the lingua franca of justice.

Although the volume of labour law has increased, then, in these various ways, it ought not to be assumed that its significance to firms and workers has increased commensurately. 'Most workers want nothing more of the law than it should leave them alone', wrote Wedderburn, famously, in 1965 (Wedderburn, 1965). Some 50 years later, the average worker might well expect rather more of the law and the protections that it affords (Pleasance et al, 2015), but they would also encounter high hurdles were they to seek to enforce what they had come to think of as their rights (Pollert, 2005; Dickens,

2012; Kirk and Busby, 2017; Kirk, 2018). With trade union membership the exception rather than the rule, especially in the private sector, and with no labour inspectorate, as such, in this country, the only option available to such a worker would be to bring an individual claim against their employer at an employment tribunal.[2] For a variety of reasons, including the financial costs of legal advice and representation, and the emotional costs of litigation, this is not an easy thing to do (Morris, 2012). In 2013, the introduction of a system of fees, payable by all claimants, had such a dramatic effect on the number of claims brought that it could be characterized as deregulation by any other name (Bogg, 2019: 196–7).[3] At the same time, the ever-increasing preference of employing organizations – entirely unchallenged, even encouraged, by the government – for casual and short-term, even zero-hours, contracts of work has meant that an ever-greater proportion of workers do not fall within the scope of employment law. The end result is a proliferation of individual workplace rights that, for the majority, are impossible or extremely difficult to enforce (Barmes, 2015: 257).

Within firms and other employer organizations, a parallel development to juridification has been the growth of HR management (HRM). For many workers, unitarist 'HRM-ism' became the primary normative framework to regulate their working relations, largely replacing collective bargaining as a mechanism for 'filling in the gaps' in routinely incomplete contracts of employment (Freedland, 2016).[4] Especially in the US, scholars have tracked the way in which HRM developed partially in response to the proliferation of employment and equality law, as new laws were understood to require new officers or departments dedicated to managing compliance (Edelman, 1992; Dobbin and Sutton, 1998). In turn, HRM exercised significant influence on the form and content of the law, as it recast legal compliance in terms of business and efficiency rationales, providing cost-effective solutions to problems of worker loyalty, engagement and productivity. The 'managerialization' of the law was then apparent when deference was paid by the judiciary to employers as expert in the intricacies of organizational operations or informal organizational cultures, with the result that the existence of compliance procedures and policies was accepted, in itself, as evidence of compliance (Edelman, 2016). In this country, it was also apparent in the proceduralization of employment law that was a feature of several of the legislative innovations of the New Labour era, as well as in so-called 'Third Way' discourse more generally (see Barmes, 2015).

The complex intertwining of the concurrent processes of juridification and managerialization raises important questions for the regulation of work and working relations (Heery, 2010). How has HRM been shaped by employment law in the UK, and vice versa? How, as 'guardians of procedure' within medium and large organizations, do HRM professionals think about employment law, and how do they communicate to workers what their legal rights are? How are workers' understandings of employment law – their 'legal consciousness' (Ewick and Silbey, 1998) – shaped, both directly and indirectly, by their experiences of HRM? Institutions like the Chartered Institute of Personnel and Development (CIPD) in the UK are major players in the construction of legal consciousness, we would argue, (re)producing social structures of inclusion and exclusion, and contributing very centrally to the constitution of the labour market. Notions of legality and understandings of what is fair, standard, 'the going rate', reasonable and so on are dominated by HR discourses of what should occur or is appropriate in light of 'market realities'. The vague collective imaginary of labour law and employment relations owes much to the discourses of HRM-ism, interlocking with a particular Third Way slant on regulation (Dukes and Kirk, 2021), or 'progressive neoliberalism', seeking equality but eschewing redistributive politics (Fraser, 2017). All that being said, it is striking the extent to which scholarship in IR and labour law has not, for the most part, been drawn closer in recent decades. In respect of these concurrent processes of juridification and managerialization, significant gaps remain in the literature that could only adequately be addressed by interdisciplinary thinking and collaboration.

Fruitful inosculation?

Today, the field of employment relations and labour law is being reconfigured at a breathless pace by the 'fissuring' of workplaces and the precarization of work (Weil, 2017). Alongside the large, bureaucratic firms invoked earlier, with high numbers of employees and formalized disciplinary, grievance, review and promotions procedures, account must also be taken of all manner of work organization, including: the platforms offering workers 'gigs'; the Amazon warehouses, supermarkets, cafes and restaurants with largely casualized, often underemployed, workforces; and the care sector, where home-care workers who were formerly the employees of local authorities are now self-employed or agency workers, or directly employed by the cared-for elderly and disabled service users (Hayes, 2017). Even within large companies and other organizations, we now frequently find tiers of two or more classes of worker: a 'core' of employees with rights and a measure of job security; and a 'periphery' of workers on fixed-term or zero-hours contracts, in respect of whom the carrot of 'employment' may readily be wielded, together with the stick of joblessness, as a means of eliciting obedient, hard work.

In making sense of these developments, it seems to us that IR and labour law scholars alike would do well to return to the shared roots of their respective disciplines. A starting point would be to recognize, as Kelly (1998) and others have urged us to do, that the decline of the major collective institutions of the Fordist era does not signal the disappearance of workers' shared interests in overcoming their vulnerability within the employment relationship. A central task for IR and labour lawyers alike remains, therefore, the identification of the kinds of laws and other institutions that might secure industrial justice (Selznick, 1969) – or post-industrial justice – in today's very varied work situations. A vital line of enquiry is, then, the connection between the experience of legally and managerially induced individualization, and the idea and practice of collectivism at work (Barmes, 2015). In light of the fissuring of workplaces and employment relations, and against the universalizing tendencies of human rights discourse, we believe that research ought to focus, in the first instance, on the single workplace or – if there is no 'place' of work – the single grouping of workers (Dukes and Streeck, 2020). Given the remoteness of the law to many workers' experiences, not only should formal legal norms be the focus of attention but also social norms: beliefs and practices shared by groups of workers concerning the organization of the work and the dividing line between the commodified and non-commodified spheres of their own lives. Here, scholars of labour law can learn from a long line of IR scholarship dealing with collective bargaining and other forms of collective deliberation, as well as from the insights that especially anthropological methods may offer into the dynamics of norm formation within small groups. Understanding the interplay of social norms with formal legal norms – the possibility for the former to shape the latter into more 'useful', directly applicable and easily enforceable sets of rules – would, then, involve consideration of the relation of these groups to, and their interaction with, society at large and its political and legal institutions. Labour law must again be studied in its particular contexts, in other words, as part of particular complexes of institutions that may be country, locality or industry specific, and changing over time (Dukes, 2019).

The founders of academic labour law had a deeply sociological understanding of the concept of law (Clark and Wedderburn, 1987; Dukes, 2014). Doctrinal 'black letter' analysis of statutory provisions was regarded as an important aspect of legal research, though one that required to be supplemented with sociological or socio-legal methods, especially in times of social and political upheaval. 'In times of sudden change', wrote Sinzheimer, 'where the old disappears and the new craves recognition, a purely technical insight in the existing legal order is not sufficient' (Sinzheimer, 1922, quoted in Kahn-Freund, 1981: 101). To understand the 'dynamic element' of the law, Sinzheimer believed, scholars had to address such questions as:

how do [legal] norms change as a result of their contact with reality ... how is the abstract content of the norm made concrete, how does it adapt itself to social reality, how does this reality influence the conceptual grouping of existing norms, and how does the spontaneous social creation of norms influence the corpus of existing norms? (Kahn-Freund, 1981: 98)

Following the legal pluralist tradition in labour law and IR means defining law broadly to include customary rules and social norms that may or may not be formalized in positive law (Selznick, 1969). Recovering the socio-legal or 'critical socio-legal' tradition in labour law means interrogating ideas of justice, normalization, legal consciousness, mobilization in relation to law, juridical concepts and the legal system (Kelly, 1998; Deakin, 2015; Dukes, 2019). For anyone with an interest in the regulation of working relations today – in the capacity of law- and rule-making institutions to secure higher levels of security and stability for working people – the inosculation, or re-entwining, of the disciplines of IR and labour law is likely to bear much fruit.

Notes

[1] In the UK, the terms 'labour law' and 'employment law' are usually understood to be synonymous.

[2] HM Revenue and Customs (HMRC) functions like a labour inspectorate in respect of employers' legal obligations to pay the National Minimum Wage. The Health and Safety Executive has an inspectorate role regarding occupational health and safety.

[3] Fees were abolished in 2017 following a legal decision in favour of the union UNISON but could be reintroduced in an amended form.

[4] Contracts of employment do not – arguably could not – attempt to regulate every aspect of the working relationship, and even central matters, such as rates of pay, are typically specified elsewhere, either in collective agreements or more usually today in HR policy documents.

References

Ackers, P. and Wilkinson, A. (2005) 'British industrial relations paradigm: a critical outline history and prognosis', *Journal of Industrial Relations*, 47: 443–56.

Barmes, L. (2015) *Bullying and Behavioural Conflict at Work: The Duality of Individual Rights*, Oxford: Oxford University Press.

Bogg, A. (2019) 'Juridification in industrial relations', in G. Gall (ed) *Handbook of the Politics of Labour, Work and Employment*, Cheltenham: Edward Elgar, pp 180–200.

Clark, J. and Wedderburn, Lord (1987) 'Juridification: a universal trend? The British experience in labour law', in G. Teubner (ed) *Juridification of Social Spheres: A Comparative Analysis in the Areas of Labor, Corporate, Antitrust and Social Welfare Law*, Berlin: Walter de Gruyter, pp 163–90.

Clegg, H.A. (1983) 'Otto Kahn-Freund and British industrial relations', in K.W. Wedderburn, R. Lewis and J. Clark (eds) *Labour Law and Industrial Relations: Building on Kahn-Freund*, Oxford: Blackwell, pp 14–28.

Crouch, C. and Pizzorno, A. (1978) *The Resurgence of Class Conflict in Western Europe since 1968: Volume I: National Studies*, New York: Springer.

Darlington, R. (2004) 'MIRS – an historical overview'. Available at: www.mirs.org.uk/history.php

Davies, P. and Freedland, M. (1993) *Labour Legislation and Public Policy*, Oxford: Clarendon Press.

Davies, P. and Freedland, M. (2002) 'National styles in labor law scholarship: the United Kingdom', *Comparative Labor Law and Policy Journal*, 23: 765–87.

Davies, P. and Freedland, M. (2007) *Towards a Flexible Labour Market*, Oxford: Oxford University Press.

Deakin, S. (2015) 'Juridical ontology: the evolution of legal form', *Historical Social Research*, 40(1): 170–84.

Dickens, L. (2012) 'Introduction', in L. Dickens (ed) *Making Employment Rights Effective: Issues of Enforcement and Compliance*, Oxford: Hart.

Dobbin, F. and Sutton, J.R. (1998) 'The strength of a weak state: the rights revolution and the rise of human resources', *American Journal of Sociology*, 104(2): 441–76.

Dukes, R. (2014) *The Labour Constitution: The Enduring Idea of Labour Law*, Oxford: Oxford University Press.

Dukes, R. (2019) 'The economic sociology of labour law', *Journal of Law and Society*, 46: 396–422.

Dukes, R. and Kirk, E. (2021) 'Law, economy and legal consciousness at work', *Northern Ireland Legal Quarterly*, 72(4): 741–70.

Dukes, R. and Streeck, W. (2020) 'Labour constitutions and occupational communities: social norms and legal norms at work', *Journal of Law and Society*, 47(4): 612–38.

Edelman, L.B. (1992) 'Legal ambiguity and symbolic structures: organizational mediation of civil rights law', *American Journal of Sociology*, 97(6): 1531–76.

Edelman, L. (2016) *Working Law: Courts, Corporations and Symbolic Civil Rights*, Chicago, IL: University of Chicago Press.

Ewick, P. and Silbey, S. (1998) *The Common Place of Law: Stories from Everyday Life*, Chicago, IL: University of Chicago Press.

Ewing, K.D. (2010) 'Foreword', in T. Novitz and C. Fenwick (eds) *Human Rights at Work*, Oxford: Hart, pp vii–xviii.

Flanders, A. (1952) 'Collective Bargaining', in A. Flanders (ed) *Trade Unions*, London: Hutchinson's University Library.

Flanders, A. and Clegg, H.A. (1954a) 'Preface', in A. Flanders and H.A. Clegg (eds) *The System of Industrial Relations in Great Britain*, Oxford: Blackwell, pp 5–6.

Flanders, A. and Clegg, H.A. (1954b) *The System of Industrial Relations in Great Britain*, Oxford: Blackwell.

Fraser, N. (2017) 'The end of progressive neoliberalism', *Dissent*. Available at: www.dissentmagazine.org/online_articles/progressive-neoliberalism-reactionary-populism-nancy-fraser

Freedland, M. (2016) 'The legal structure of the contact of employment', in M. Freedland, A. Bogg, D. Cabrelli, H. Collins, N. Countouris, A.C.L. Davies, S. Deakin and J. Prassl (eds) *The Contract of Employment*, Oxford: Oxford University Press, pp 28–51.

Hayes, L. (2017) *Stories of Care: A Labour of Law: Gender and Class at Work*, London: Palgrave.

Heery, E. (2010) 'Debating employment law: responses to juridification', in P. Blyton, E. Heery and P.J. Turnbull (eds) *Reassessing the Employment Relationship*, London: Palgrave Macmillan, pp 71–96.

Kahn-Freund, O. (1954) 'Legal framework', in A. Flanders and H.A. Clegg (eds) *The System of Industrial Relations in Great Britain*, Oxford: Blackwell.

Kahn-Freund, O. (1981) 'Hugo Sinzheimer 1875–1945', in R. Lewis and J. Clark (eds) *Labour Law and Politics in the Weimar Republic*, Oxford: Blackwell, pp73–107.

Kaufman, B.E. (2014) 'History of the British industrial relations field reconsidered: getting from the Webbs to the new employment relations paradigm, *British Journal of Industrial Relations*, 52(1): 1–31.

Kelly, J. (1998) *Rethinking Industrial Relations: Mobilization, Collectivism and Long Waves*, London: Routledge.

Kirk, E. (2018) 'The "problem" with the employment tribunal system: reform, rhetoric and realities for the clients of Citizens' Advice Bureaux', *Work, Employment and Society*, 32(6): 975–91.

Kirk, E. and Busby, N. (2017) 'Led up the tribunal path? Employment disputes, legal consciousness and trust in the protection of law', *Oñati Socio-Legal Series*, 7(7): 1397–420.

Morris, G. (2012) 'The development of statutory employment rights in Britain and enforcement mechanisms', in L. Dickens (ed) *Making Employment Rights Effective: Issues of Enforcement and Compliance*, Oxford: Hart, pp 7–28.

Pleasance, P., Balmber, N.J. and Denvir, C. (2015) 'Wrong about rights: public knowledge of key areas of consumer, housing and employment law in England and Wales', *Modern Law Review*, 80(5): 836–59.

Pollert, A. (2005) 'The unorganised worker: the decline in collectivism and new hurdles to individual employment rights', *Industrial Law Journal*, 34(3): 217–38.

Selznick, P. (1969) *Law, Society, and Industrial Justice*, New York: Russell Sage.

Simpson, B. (2001) 'The changing face of British collective labour law', *Oxford Journal of Legal Studies*, 21(4): 705–17.

Sinzheimer, H. (1922) 'On the sociological and positivistic method in the discipline of labour law', *Arbeitsrecht*, 9: 187–98.

Taylor, S. and Emir, A. (2006) *Employment Law: An Introduction*, Oxford: Oxford University Press.

Voskiterian, H. (2010) 'The intellectual and institutional development of BUIRA: a 60 year retrospective', BUIRA. Available at: www.buira.net/the-intellectual-and-institutional-development-of-buira-a-60-years-retrospective/

Waddington, J., Müller, T. and Vandaele, K. (2019) 'Setting the scene: collective bargaining under neoliberalism', in T. Müller, K. Vandaele and J. Waddington (eds) *Collective Bargaining in Europe: Towards an Endgame*, Brussels: ETUI, pp 1–32.

Webb, S. and Webb, B. (1897) *Industrial Democracy*, London: Longmans, Green.

Wedderburn, K.W. (1965) *The Worker and the Law*, Harmondsworth: Pelican.

Wedderburn, K.W. (1971) *The Worker and the Law*, 2nd edn, Harmondsworth: Pelican.

Weil, D. (2017) *The Fissured Workplace*, Cambridge, MA: Harvard University Press.

10

Conflict and Industrial Action

Gregor Gall

Introduction

After the uptick in strike activity from the summer of 2022 onwards, it may seem a strange question to ask but, nonetheless: what if there were no strikes in any of the years of the rest of the decade in Britain? What would this mean, and what would its overall significance be? Asking these questions at the very outset helps to get straight to the heart of, arguably, the most salient issue for those studying conflict at work in the present period. This is that the existence of conflict[1] within the employment relationship and the expression of that conflict, in whatever form, are not synonymous with each other. They should merely be thought of as overlapping circles in a Venn diagram. Put even more bluntly, the likes of strikes are but the symptoms of conflict and not its causes.[2] Therefore, it is possible to have conflict in the employment relationship without any overt expressions of that conflict, mostly obviously, in the form of strikes. Of course, that does mean that it is often harder to then spot the manifestations of conflict without the overt signs of it. Under capitalism, the primary axis of conflict in the employment relationship is between the material interests of capital (employers and management) and those of labour (employees and workers). Alongside these material interests, power and ideology are the other principal and related components in the employment relationship and thus wider economy and society. They form a mutually reinforcing troika within a system based upon the drive to accumulate profits (surplus value) through the exploitation of labour and in competition with other units of capital.

Asking these initial questions about strikes is not an abstract exercise, as will be argued shortly. Asking them helps form the starting point for trying to cast some fresh light on some age-old issues about conflict at work by asking a number of other questions. One of these is: 'Why do those studying industrial relations still think that spending time looking at the conflict between capital and labour within the employment relationship under capitalism is worthwhile?' Another is: 'Why do the most important expressions of conflict predominantly take collective forms?' Some others are: 'Do workers need to be organized and in unions to strike?'; 'What form have innovations in the expression of conflict taken from workers and employers, and why are these relatively limited in extent?'; and 'How dangerous for capital is the expression of conflict by labour?'

From strike wave to strike drought

Notwithstanding the upturn in strike activity from mid-2022 into 2023 over the cost-of-living crisis, the situation in Britain is such that the withering away of the strike is becoming an ever-greater prospect if the contemporary and overall downward trajectory is continued. It is likely that the COVID-19 pandemic has further accentuated this.[3] Although subject to politically inspired exaggeration from both the Right and Left, Britain has experienced substantial strike waves in the past, with the last ones to date taking place from the late 1960s to the late 1970s, where tens of millions of days were not worked. Yet, even these were dwarfed by the size of the strikes in 1921 and 1926, where hundreds of millions of days were not worked. Consequently, according to the Office of National Statistics (ONS), in 2018, the last year for which there is presently complete data, there were just 273,000 working days not worked due to strikes, the sixth-lowest annual total since records began in 1891.[4] Just 39,000 workers were involved in these strikes, the second-lowest figure since records for workers involved began in 1893, and just 81 stoppages took place, the second-lowest figure since records for stoppages began in 1930. Provisional data for 2019 show that there were 234,000 days not worked due to strikes. Due to the impact of COVID-19, there has been a significant delay in more recent annual data becoming available. In a few years from now, it will be possible to see whether 2022 and 2023 represented turning points or just mere bumps in the downward-running road to continued quiescence (as was the likes of November 2011, with its one-day public sector pension strike). However, what we do know so far is that between June 2022 and February 2023, 3.014 million days were not worked due to strikes.

Strikes are but one form of expression or manifestation of conflict and do not constitute conflict itself. The same is true of other forms. So, if in 2024 or 2025, for example, there were no strikes or almost no strikes, would this mean that an alignment of interests between labour and capital had been created, leading to industrial harmony, where the odd strike could be put down to some kind of aberrant deviance? Could it be that human resource management was no longer inhumane resource management and that employers really did now treat their workers as their most valuable assets and not annoying costs? Or, could this also mean that neoliberalism has, over the last four decades, fundamentally reconfigured capitalism so that conflict between capital and labour is no longer central to any employment relationship (for reasons of workers objectively and subjectively becoming 'capitalistic')?

Before believing that affirmative answers could be reached in any case here, as well as questioning how deep-seated and permanent this new harmony was, there could be other plausible explanations for this state of affairs. It could mean that workers had no need to strike because employers caved in at the first slight hint of a strike threat or strike ballot. It could mean that the state had intervened in industrial relations to create a compulsory arbitration system, so that workers no longer needed to engage in strike action in order to be effective in gaining their bargaining goals. It could also mean that the overall state of the labour market was such that workers feared being replaced by others if they struck. In this sense, the quiescence was a very reluctant one. Of these, only the last one is a serious contender for seeking to explain, in part, the absence of the level of strikes we might otherwise anticipate.

A sociologically informed perspective, influenced by mobilization theory (Kelly, 1998), would first and foremost highlight one issue above all others. This would be to ask: what organizational means do workers have available to them by which to strike? In doing so, this perspective would suggest that the absence of strikes might merely indicate no more than a situation where workers are unable to either collectively articulate their grievances or to seek to redress and resolve these via strikes. This might arise due to, among other things: a decline in union membership and atrophy of workplace unionism, so that workers are not organized to do so; strikes being restricted by various legal measures; and union leaderships not being supportive of their members wishing to strike. From here, this perspective would examine the process by which workers consider whether to mobilize in order to express their conflict of interests, such as what attributions could be made as to the cause of their grievances, and what windows of opportunity exist to be utilized (such as tight labour markets or points of employer vulnerability). This would be to examine whether the necessary building blocks were present to allow the 'anger → hope → action' phenomenon to come into being.

However, a sociological approach to the absence of strikes would also examine the issue of 'method displacement' (see, for example, Gall and Kirk, 2018). There are many other alternatives to traditional striking, such as use of ballots for industrial action as bargaining chips, industrial action short of striking (like work-to-rule, go-slows and overtime bans), partial performance of duties and 'mass sickies' (or 'duvet days'), where sickness absence is used as a de facto strike when no sickness or illness exists. The problem here is that reliable time-series data on these other phenomena do not usually exist, largely because they are difficult to capture statistically (Gall and Kirk, 2018). This is even more so with other expressions of disquiet and resistance like pilfering and sabotage, which can take more individualized and atomized forms.

Who and what causes strikes?

The preceding discussion helps explain why there is such a focus upon strike activity as the premier expression of conflict. Compared to other forms of industrial action, strikes are relatively easy to identify, as they are visible internally within an organization, usually because work stops and has an immediate impact (even if not a catastrophically disruptive one on the employer's operations). They are often visible externally too, with physical picketing and mainstream and new media campaigns being utilized. This means that they can be measured. But who causes strikes (and other forms of industrial action)? Before answering this, it is worth noting that employers can take their own forms of industrial action against workers. The lockout, where workers are not allowed to return to work even when they wish to, is the most obvious form, while sacking strikers, victimizations of union representatives (through sackings) and punitive divestment (closing workplaces or not making further investments) are other forms. However, compared to strikes by workers, they are relatively uncommon, lockouts especially.

A 'common-sense' logic suggests that it takes 'two to tango', so that both parties – labour and capital – are equally to 'blame' for the industrial disharmony. This kind of view is often reinforced by politicians and governments who call upon both parties to be 'reasonable' and to 'get back to the negotiating table' in order to reach an agreement to prevent or end a strike. However, given its dominant right-wing bias, the media is much more prone to suggest that workers and their unions are the cause of strikes. After all, in the case of strikes, it is workers and their unions that take the actions, being said to 'walk out' from their workplaces while management ask them not to do so and stay in their offices working when they do. However, contrary to these perspectives, employers and their managers are the creators of conflict. In the employment relationship under capitalism, it is capital that creates the employment relationship itself, no matter the subsequent terms for the exploitation of labour. This gives capital the power of initiative in terms of pursuing its material interests. Furthermore, in addition to this, capital has the resources (financial and organizational) to carry out what actions flow from its power of initiative. Consequently, workers are always cast as the reactive and weaker party,[5] responding to what management do as management seek to chase profits by cutting costs, increasing productivity and so on. This might be by changing working practices, changing working hours or freezing pay rates. In this context, strikes and the like are a response to this, where the material interests of labour and capital clash, and labour seeks to resist the new terms of exploitation. The relationship is necessarily a relationship of exploitation and oppression to produce surplus value (or profit), and not one of even interdependence and mutual respect. All this may sound rather counterintuitive to many, especially to unitarists (see Chapter 2), given that the managerial prerogative, based upon the laws of property ownership and associated ideology, gives management the right to manage and, with that, the supposed legitimacy to manage.

Why is conflict still studied?

So, with overt forms of conflict expression in decline, why do those studying industrial relations still think that studying conflict between capital and labour is worthwhile? One reason is that forms and expressions of conflict have changed. For example, with weakened workplace unionism and further restrictions on collective industrial action, political campaigning – like the leverage campaign, which seeks to put pressure on other stakeholders through reputational damage – has become more prevalent than ever before. Another is that worker resistance as an expression of the conflict of interests can represent an obstacle to productivity and profitability. However, there are other reasons. The expression of conflict as a symptom of the underlying conflict itself is important for industrial relations academics for two particular reasons. The first is that its shows that capital has not achieved complete physical and mental control over labour. Although there is a tendency among some industrial relations academics to wrongly proclaim that 'two swallows make a summer', that is, a small number of strikes represent a manifest turning point, industrial relations academics can still point to worker resistance as an evident phenomenon. To do so is, then, to reject any purchase of unitarism, putting industrial relations academics into the camps of pluralism or radicalism (see Chapter 2). Indeed, some radicals and Marxists would insist that this is testament to the innate and unceasing conflict between labour and capital under capitalism. Edwards (1986) denoted this as a 'structured antagonism'. The second is that the intellectual framework of many industrial relations academics is something approximating to a radical one, and this has a particularly important value-laden ramification. It means that workers' resistance is regarded as an important wellspring of workers' self-activity that is capable of restricting the behaviour of capital and, with that, a possible source of creating overall progressive social change, mostly obviously, in the form of revolutionary socialism.

Innovations in action

The term 'strike' is believed to derive from the action of sailors in London in 1768 who 'struck', or removed, the topgallant sails of the merchant ships they worked on, thus crippling the ships from sailing. However, strikes themselves date from very early pre-capitalist times, such as the artisans of the Royal Necropolis at Deir el-Medina walking off their jobs because they had not been paid in 1152 BC. The first general strike in the world was not in 1842 in England – the Chartist strike – but in 1820 in Scotland – the 'Radical War' of the Calton weavers. Subsequent to this, strikes experienced little in the way of innovation save a few developments like the sit-down strike, as used by US auto-workers in the late 1930s, so that workers did not put themselves outside the workplace and in a difficult position of trying to control the factory from outside as a result of 'walking out'. 'Wildcat' and 'unofficial' strikes are simply those strikes that do not abide by established procedures (whether union rules, agreements with employers or state regulations).

There are, however, some historically more recent innovations worth noting. One was the Upper Clyde Shipbuilders (UCS) work-in of June 1971 to October 1972, which secured the future of the yards by compelling state intervention against the wishes of the then Conservative government. The work-in comprised workers taking over the yards and completing the orders for ships themselves in a form of self-management in order to demonstrate the viability of the yards. This new tactic was chosen because a strike would have put workers outside the yards, while an occupation would be difficult to sustain over the long term. Bogusly self-employed courier workers for the likes of Deliveroo and Uber Eats in Britain have recently developed the tactics of 'switching off the app' so that they can, in effect, mount a wildcat strike where they do not need to ballot for such action because they are not, in the main, legally employed workers. They have also developed the tactic of boycotting deliveries for particular companies while continuing to work for others in order to maximize pressure on specific companies while also maintaining some earnings for themselves. These recent developments have run in train with leverage approaches that go beyond merely demonstrating outside company annual general meetings (AGMs) or chief executives' homes. Here, there is a 'total war' approach of targeting clients and suppliers upstream and downstream with reputational damage, using employment tribunals (see Chapter 9) and other legal remedies to set conducive collective precedents, and engaging in disruptive 'flashmob' protests, as well as forms of traditional industrial action (like strikes). Outside of Britain, suicide by jumping off company buildings or self-immolation are not uncommon in a number of countries in the Far East and Asia, and neither is rioting as a form of action to precipitate collective bargaining in the likes of Indonesia. For a time, 'bossnapping' was common in France. These tactics reflect situations like the absence of independent unions and the severe difficulties in organizing lawful strikes.

What is surprising is that with the ever-increasing reliance upon more sophisticated information and communication technologies, as well as upon more complex and fragile supply chains, sabotage has not become rekindled as a mass modern weapon in workers' armoury (see Gall, 2013). Of course, capital has developed means to prevent such sabotage, and workers will not be willing to openly publicize such actions for fear of reprisal. Yet, nonetheless, the absence of this type of sabotage is still highly notable. Indeed, it would seem that the withdrawal of the willingness to labour has become so deeply etched into the psyche of workers that other means of disruption find it hard to register in workers' collective imagination. For example, rather than not doing something by workers withdrawing their labour, little consideration of deliberately doing the 'wrong' thing seems to have taken place. This might be not doing the right thing at the right time, such as front-line service workers charging the incorrect prices for the goods and services that the employer they work for provides and sells.

Why do expressions of conflict predominantly take collective and unionized forms?

It is difficult to say what the balance between individual, atomized actions, on the one hand, and collective actions, on the other, is given the aforementioned paucity of data. Nonetheless, it does appear that collective forms of the expression of conflict are predominant. Why is this likely to be the case? Although in law, the employment contract is between a unit of capital and an individual worker, the nature of work is overwhelmingly a collective activity and collective experience. For example, pay rises (or cuts) are often applied to all non-management employees in the same way and at the same time. However, more than that, if workers are to seek to meet the capitalists that employ them on anything approaching equal terms, then they must aggregate themselves and their resources. When it comes to taking action, that logically means taking collective action. Therefore, 'unity is strength', though only really when it is unity in creating leverage through action, and while unions are not the only form of collective associations, they are by far and away the most common kind. This is because they make a fist of independence from the employer through self-reliance, so that they have the resources to organize, represent and bargain with. Worker associations that are not unions as such are common in the information technology sector, with the Tech Workers Coalition being the main example.[6] They are also common in the 'gig' economy sector, especially in the US (Nahmias, 2021), where a capital–labour relationship exists despite the bogus status of self-employment for workers. The aforementioned logic of collective association also means that the vast majority of strikes are organized by unions. One recent exception was the walkout in November 2018 by 20,000 workers at Google. Here, collective organization developed in train with the preparation for the strike. In both these information technology examples, unions are emerging from these embryonic organizations, whether that means joining existing communication worker unions or establishing new ones (like the Alphabet Workers' Union at Google in 2021).

Need capital be worried by industrial action?

How dangerous are the primary expressions of conflict at work for the interests of the established order outside of revolutionary upheavals like those in the post-war period: Hungary in 1956, France in 1968, Chile in 1972, Portugal in 1974, Iran in 1979 and Poland in 1980? 'Not very' is the straight and simple answer. Taking strikes as the most obvious expression of conflict and with the exception of prolonged periods of general strikes, strikes in themselves are not a fundamental challenge to management, capital and capitalism. Moreover, seldom do they in themselves have a transformative potential by, for example, making the scales fall off the eyes of workers so that, to use a phrase, they 'see capitalism for what it really is' and then move from being a class in themselves to a class for themselves. Strikes are temporary phenomena over partial aspects of management's power and control in the employment relationship. They are more often than not about 'pounds and pence' or the terms of being fired rather than about management's right to fire.[7] So, what about occupations of workplaces, where managers are expelled or even kidnapped and property confiscated? Such instances were relatively widespread in France during 2009–10. Even here, the objective is seldom to completely take over the enterprise or workplace (see Gall, 2011). In France, these instances were about creating the bargaining leverage to impose upon capital the continuation of previous capitalist exploitation, namely, employment upon existing terms and conditions. An interesting exception might be the example of the 'recovered enterprises' in Argentina in the early 2000s, where to save their jobs under something approximating to existing terms and conditions, workers took over the factories they worked in and turned them into cooperatives. Many of these are still in operation today. However, they exist like other cooperatives, not so much as 'islands of socialism in seas of capitalism' but as alternative capitalist enterprises operating within capitalism. This follows the trajectory established by the Lip watch factory workers in France taking over the factory they worked in from 1973 until 1983. All that said, strikes and occupations are the more potent forms of workers' resistance compared to misbehaviour and deviance at work (see Richards, 2008).

Conclusion

Under capitalism, conflict in the employment relationship does not just take place within the employment relationship itself. As capitalism is, first and foremost, an economic system, this conflict seeps out into the wider polity and society because the basis of society under capitalism is its economic system. This means that conflict over work does not just take place within the workplace. Therefore, the substance of the conflict within the employment relationship has given rise to the creation of political formations, mostly obviously, social-democratic parties to represent the interests of labour, often through unions establishing these parties.[8] Of course, conflict is not the only main feature of employment relations under capitalism; for some, the temporary alignment of interests between labour and capital in one enterprise is possible against labour and capital in another. This need not ever take the shape of formalized partnership agreements. All that said, the study of conflict speaks to the long-standing, usually implicit, concerns of researchers and writers. While this chapter began by considering the case of Britain, the issues discussed are generic to other similar industrialized economies in the northern and southern hemispheres. However, if conflict is (still) innate and inherent to the employment relationship and the relationship between capital and labour under capitalism, then many would expect there to be many more overt expressions of this conflict, especially from the side of labour as the exploited and oppressed party. The lack of these overt expressions has led some to conclude that secular change has taken place. However, this is myopic and merely reinforces the strength of the case for examining whether the means are available to workers to express the conflict they are subject to and part of.

Notes

[1] Often denoted as 'conflict at work' and 'workplace conflict'.

[2] This is the case even where the conduct of a strike and its associated paraphernalia (like picketing) can become contentious issues in themselves. Here, they merely aggravate an existing conflict.

[3] This is as a result of redundancies despite furlough schemes, depressed economic demand and the disorganization inflicted upon unions though pandemic social restrictions. As Office of National Statistics (ONS) monthly strike data run some 15 months behind 'live' strikes, the scale of the possible impact will not be known for some time. This is all the more so given the suspension of data collection by the ONS from January 2020 to June 2022.

[4] The education sector accounted for 66 per cent of all working days lost, mainly due to disputes involving employees of universities.

[5] Even though unions have full-time staffs and some employers grant facility time, workers have to work to organize themselves in addition to their work. Management's job is to manage, so its work here is done within its work time.

[6] For reasons of workers seeing themselves as professionals that do not seem to need unions.

[7] This is often termed 'economism', indicating the absence of a fundamental challenge to capital.

[8] The hegemony of neoliberalism has meant that most social-democratic parties are now social democratic in name only.

References

Edwards, P. (1986) *Conflict at Work: A Materialist Analysis of Workplace Relations*, Oxford: Blackwell.

Gall, G. (2011) 'Contemporary workplace occupations in Britain: stimuli, dynamics and outcomes', *Employee Relations*, 33(6): 607–23.

Gall, G. (2013) 'Introduction', in G. Gall (ed) *New Forms and Expressions of Conflict at Work*, Palgrave: Basingstoke, pp 1–6.

Gall, G. and Kirk, E. (2018) 'Striking out in a new direction? Strikes and the displacement thesis', *Capital and Class*, 42(2): 195–203.

Kelly, J. (1998) *Rethinking Industrial Relations: Mobilisation, Collectivism and Long Waves*, London: Routledge.

Nahmias, G. (2021) *Innovations in Collective Action in the Labor Movement: Organizing Workers beyond the NLRA and the Business Union*, MIT Work of the Future Working Paper 13–2021, Cambridge, MA: Massachusetts Institute of Technology.

Richards, J. (2008) 'The many approaches to organisational misbehaviour: a review, map and research agenda', *Employee Relations*, 30(6): 653–78.

11

Exploring 'New' Forms of Work Organization: The Case of Parcel Delivery in the UK

Sian Moore, Kirsty Newsome and Stefanie Williamson

Introduction

Reflecting the surge in online delivery under COVID-19, UK government figures show significant growth in logistics, warehouse and transport jobs during the pandemic (ONS, 2021a). Typically non-standard, low paid and closely monitored, the character of jobs in this sector raises questions about flexible labour markets and notions of 'self-employment'. Terms including 'precarity', 'gig' and 'platform' work now arguably dominate the narrative within the field of work and industrial relations. Yet, the wider academic discourse on 'flexible' work has been with us far longer: Pollert (1988) dismantled flexibility, along with the concept of dual labour markets, in 1988. Her analysis revealed the way in which contemporary analysts were prone to conflate under flexibility the distinct processes of job enlargement, effort intensification and cost controls. The same tendency can be seen in recent accounts that invoke flexibility to mask management prerogative, work degradation and job insecurity. This chapter reviews 'new' forms of work organization through the lens of parcel delivery. It explores notions of flexibility and work autonomy, and focuses on the contradictory relationship between digital technology and self-employment.

At the end of the supply chain: parcel delivery and flexible labour markets

'Essential' parcel-delivery workers in the UK are particularly emblematic of work in the contemporary economy. With the growth of online retailing and business models embracing a myriad of subcontracted supply chains, transformations in parcel delivery have been directed at securing more exacting, demanding and time-critical levels of service delivery at minimum cost. Increasingly complex information technology (IT) systems provide coherence to fragmented employment systems, as well as tracking the movement of parcels under the gaze of the final customer. Amazon and other large retailers entice their customers with 'free and immediate' delivery, which relies upon the supply of flexible and closely monitored labour at minimum cost. Overall, the result is an increasingly competitive market for parcel delivery companies, dominated by intense supply chain pressures and fissured workplaces resulting in a degradation of work for parcel-delivery workers (Moore and Newsome, 2018).

For delivery companies, the time incurred by non-delivery represents a crucial cost. The use of so-called 'self-employed' delivery workers paid by delivery removes these costs, as labour time incurred in non-delivery is unpaid. Self-employment removes employment rights and social protection in the form of sick and holiday pay and pensions. The 24/7 nature of delivery is paid for at flat piece rates, with no notion of unsocial hours for workers while accommodating the work–life balance of consumers. Under COVID-19, dependent self-employment represented the ultimate transfer of risk to the individual worker, with no organizational responsibility for health and safety, while the absence of sick pay discouraged workers from taking time off when they or their households were symptomatic. Government statistics reveal that for males, drivers were at a higher risk of COVID-19 deaths than other occupations (ONS, 2021d). A YouGov survey found that the public perceived delivery workers as vulnerable: just under one third said that they had ordered non-essential items despite thinking that delivery workers had a 50:50 chance of catching COVID-19, while taxi drivers and ride-share workers (such as Uber) were seen as particularly susceptible to COVID-19. A further aspect of self-employment has been underlined by COVID-19: ease of entry to the labour market. Job loss and furlough during the pandemic may have encouraged an influx of workers into the delivery sector, with the potential to drive down volume for existing workers, leading to longer working hours to ensure income.

The proliferation of online delivery has raised further issues about UK flexible employment models, particularly the fiction of 'self-employment'. Pollert (1988: 43) noted that 'flexibility' has been a handy legitimator precisely because of its 'all-purpose resistance to precise definition'. Her polemic challenged the notion of dual labour markets – the core and peripheral workforce – and it is instructive that labour platforms have been characterized as a step in the continuing dualization of the labour market rooted in economic globalization and the technical innovations of the 1970s and 1980s (Collier et al, 2017). Yet, in calling for flexibility to be historically situated, Pollert (1988) warned against assertions that segmentation is a departure from previously homogenized internal markets. She emphasized generalized attacks on working conditions for all workers, characterized by neoliberal restructuring, work intensification and rationalization.

Contemporary debates regarding flexible working have been closely allied to the growth of non-standard forms of employment following the 2008 crisis. More specifically, with the emergence of 'new' forms of working (for example, zero-hour contracts), questions have been raised regarding the 'one-sided' nature of flexibility and the adoption of business models predicated upon low pay and exploitative business practices based upon growing levels of workplace insecurity (Low Pay Commission, 2018; Moore et al, 2018). In essence, 'one-sided flexibility' exposes the power imbalance at the heart of the employment relationship and the capacity for employers to reduce the employment relationship to a disposable transaction, at the core of which is the aim of cost minimization. More specifically, extending the ideological dimensions of notions of flexibility, one-sided flexibility can manifest itself in several ways relating to contractual status, as well as the organization and experience of work. Drawing on evidence from parcel delivery, the next section explores the dynamics of self-employment in the contemporary economy.

Embedding flexibility: contractual status in parcel delivery

The case of parcel-delivery workers illustrates how non-standard work (in this case, dependent self-employment) is intimately entwined within wider business models and employment practices. Previous research exploring how supply-chain pressures are reflected in the contractual status of workers highlighted three interconnected tiers of contractual status (Moore and Newsome, 2018). The first constitutes directly employed drivers based in large parcel-delivery companies, in which employment relations are framed by extant collective agreements with a history of bargaining over terms and conditions. The second tier are 'self-employed' owner-drivers paid by piece-rate pay and often based in depots working alongside directly employed drivers. The third tier is so-called 'lifestyle couriers', also technically self-employed but operating from home using their own vehicles.

All sources of labour power may be present within a single enterprise. While directly employed drivers have fixed hours and hourly rates, self-employed drivers are paid by piece rate, based upon the number of deliveries or drops. The key advantage of owner-drivers for the companies is increased levels of volume and the transfer of risk through the removal of the costs of non-delivery. Moore and Newsome (2018) highlight that in one case-study organization, directly employed drivers had a target of 70–80 drops per day. By contrast, owner-drivers were expected to achieve in the region of 120–130 drops per day. Owner-drivers were reported to receive £1.65 per parcel-delivery stop and £2 for collections or pick-ups. Rates per drop for home couriers varied from 85p to £1 per item. Dependent self-employed workers were only paid for deliveries. The working day included failed deliveries, for which they received no pay, with no extra payment for reattempts to deliver, timed deliveries or the sorting of parcels and loading of vans prior to delivery.

In addition, the research illustrated that if self-employed drivers were sick, wanted to take a holiday or were faced with any family emergency, they would be required to provide substitute cover for their route or they would be charged by the company for the costs of a replacement agency worker and may also be fined. Failure to deliver the required parcels (often within specified delivery slots) could result in the immediate removal of work. As one respondent highlighted: "You live in threat of them saying, 'No parcels, that's it.' You've got nothing, and that's what they threaten you with all the time: 'We'll just take your parcels.'" In parcel delivery, self-employment translates into the removal of basic rights, safeguards on hours, holiday, and sickness entitlements (Moore and Newsome, 2018; Newsome et al, 2018b).

The 'fiction' of self-employment: exploring autonomy and preference

While evidence highlights that the standard employment model continues to predominate in the UK, it has been partially subverted by a growing array of non-standard or insecure employment models. Non-standard forms of employment refer to varying contractual and non-contractual relationships commonly characterized by variable and irregular hours (Moore et al, 2017). Around 15 per cent of the UK population was self-employed in 2020 (ONS, 2020), with 6 per cent of the UK workforce estimated to be in dependent self-employment in 2015. Those in self-employment were more likely to be men, while there was variation by race and ethnicity, for example, 25 per cent of Pakistani workers were self-employed (ONS, 2021c).

The debate about dependent self-employment is rooted in narratives of flexibility and 'preference', as manifested in the Taylor Review of modern working practices (Taylor et al, 2017), and the academic literature similarly explores the capacity for temporal flexibility and control (see, for example, the *Industrial Relations Journal* special issue published in 2018 on the Taylor Review on modern working practices). The academic literature on gender has long problematized the notion of 'preference' in relation to women workers. In terms of self-employment, preference is similarly problematic, and the notion of 'autonomy' that self-employment implies is important to workers, even when diminished by the technological surveillance of work.

Josserand and Kaine's (2019) study of ride-share drivers in Australia illuminates how they construct self-narratives that resolve the contradictions between their occupational identity and the material reality of work. Such constructions include presenting their work as 'only a temporary episode or a marginal activity', as well as the assertion of freedom and independence. Similarly, Harvey et al's (2017) study of self-employed personal trainers suggests that such contractual relationships may give rise to the overestimation of not only autonomy but also income. Interrogation of the notion of worker preference for flexible work (or non-standard contracts) has been exposed in terms of their limited autonomy over working time and unpredictable work–life balance, undermined by the need to comply with the temporal rhythms of customer demand (Ravenelle, 2019; see also Rosenblat, 2018; Griesbach et al, 2019; Gregory, 2021). The insecurity of such contracts may be veiled by regular hours and shifts that imply permanent work. Sun et al's (2023) research on food-delivery workers in China shows that riders were faced with 'the choice' of moving from previously flexible hours to full-time and fixed schedules in order to secure more orders from the platform and to earn a decent wage, despite being paid at a piece rate calculated on the number of fulfilled orders rather than log-on time. Their reliance on a platform's labour-management regime meant intensified digital monitoring and extended, rather than fragmented, working hours.

Evidence from parcel-delivery workers reveals that beneath the appeal of apparent flexibility, work as a 'lifestyle courier' involves chronic uncertainty and high levels of unpredictability over hours of work and ultimately pay (Moore and Newsome, 2018; Newsome et al, 2018a; 2018b). Self-employed 'home couriers' attracted by the promise of flexible hours and days of work, in reality, had little choice over the number of days worked and the timing of working hours. One driver reported, 'you don't have the freedom of your day', as she felt compelled to work seven days a week on two contracts, and further reported: 'it's taken over our lives and the stress and anxiety and the fatigue that it causes is huge and I just feel that we're missing life' (Moore et al, 2018: 411). Other lifestyle couriers reported high levels of unpredictability and uncertainty regarding the number of parcels that they would be required to deliver each day, which directly impacted upon levels of income, which could fluctuate significantly, causing daily stress and anxiety. One driver outlined the tension each day:

> You're talking insecure work, you don't how many (parcels) are coming. We could all get up tomorrow, and we could have a hundred. That is a good day's work, we'll all be above minimum wage. But we could also get up and have ten. You live day to day. The wage I am on, we'll live, but it won't pay the bills. (Newsome et al, 2018a: 90)

In addition, as self-employed drivers were on piece rates, many reported on the high levels of unpaid labour they were required to undertake daily. Each morning lifestyle couriers engaged in the daily routine of checking, scanning and loading parcels onto their vehicles; depending on the volume, this could take up to two hours. In addition, non-deliveries or second attempts received no additional payment. Finally, lifestyle couriers also highlighted that time deliveries (the requirement to deliver parcels at specifics times of the day) also received no extra payment. On the contrary, if deliveries were made outside the time stipulated to customers, drivers would be fined. This meant that drivers often faced the prospect of waiting in their vans by the side of the road until the exact delivery window stipulated to the customer. As one driver reported: 'everyone's time is important, except for mine' (Moore and Newsome, 2018: 412).

Digital monitoring: diminishing autonomy

Discussion of digital and automated technologies has been linked to rather speculative arguments about the future of work. Some writers see unlimited possibilities for robots to displace labour and talk with confidence of a post-work future (Mason, 2015; Bastani, 2019). In less grandiose terms, others fixate on the possibilities for more creative and autonomous forms of working. These accounts are often at odds with detailed empirical studies of the diffusion of technology, which reveal the continuing salience of 'institutions, interests and power' (Lloyd and Payne, 2021: 110). From this perspective, a micro focus on historically specific sectoral conditions must be the starting point for a serious assessment of the character and (uneven) impacts of technology.

Gig work – the focus of much recent research – is not in and of itself indicative of a radical transformation in the social relations of work. Indeed, it has elements in common with earlier forms of capitalist work organization, such as the putting-out system and latter-day forms of subcontracting. The significant difference is the way in which technology has been harnessed by capital to further subjugate labour. For gig workers, technology (the platform and algorithmic systems) is utilized to direct how, where and when to work, and, correspondingly, to collect data on performance outcomes. Yet, algorithmic management is not confined to gig workers per se. A recent study by the Institute for the Future of Work thus speaks of the 'Amazonian era' to encapsulate the features of a wider business model in which the workforce is managed by algorithms. This creates an environment of almost total surveillance, collecting and processing data about every aspect of working life in real time. This is used to drive people to complete more tasks in less time, intensifying their work. Standards set by the system are then used to evaluate and manage performance, incentivize or penalize workers, and grant or deny them access to stable work contracts (IFOW, 2021: 9). Growing references to 'digital Taylorism' thus reflect the capacity for the real-time measurement of labour performance, which creates the capacity for labour optimization, removing the porosity of the working day and thus reducing costs. The evidence from parcel-delivery workers, our main concern, offers a sobering and far-from-unique case of the scope for degraded work patterns in the UK. The exercise of management prerogative through the digital monitoring of delivery workers further unveils the fiction of self-employment, highlighting what can only be regarded as a tightly 'managed workforce' (Griesbach et al, 2019).

Digital technologies in the logistics sector provide the necessary coherence to a business model based upon fragmented supply chains, subcontracted relationships and fissured workplaces, with an array of associated employment practices and contracts (Cowen, 2014; Sowers, 2017). These technologies have the capacity to track the movement of products in a seamless flow from production to points of passage, gateways, ports and, finally, the last-mile delivery. More specifically, for last-mile parcel-delivery workers, the transformations in logistics technology have the capacity not only to track the movement of the parcel but also to correspondingly monitor the performance of labour. Gregson (2017), referring to the growth in self-employment in lorry drivers (comparable atomized workers), contrasts the once-nomadic lorry driver as 'king of the road' with the current tracing of repetitive spatial movements via Global Positioning System (GPS) tracking, with the opportunity for real-time monitoring. These algorithmic tools and routing software not only speed up circulation (value in motion) but also simultaneously offer the possibility of closer and tighter performance management (Newsome, 2015).

For parcel-delivery workers, the introduction of hand-held personal digital assistants (PDAs) has also had a fundamental impact on the nature of their work. These devices render the last mile of delivery more transparent by providing senders and their recipients 'sight' of an item's real-time progress and expected delivery time. The routing software incorporated into the devices, which dictates predetermined routes for delivery, effectively removes driver autonomy and discretion. Lifestyle couriers reported increasing levels of monitoring and surveillance, with the micromanagement of how and when they deliver their parcels. Respondents reported that the growing levels of monitoring and surveillance, allied to punitive performance measures, were seemingly at odds with their self-employed status (Moore and Newsome, 2018).

Such real-time monitoring of effort represents an area of growing contestation within the work relationship. In the case of parcel-delivery workers in organizations where collective agreements were in place, negotiations took place to restrict the use of data generated through the digital devices for the purpose of surveillance and discipline. Agreements specify the limits to the intensity of work and regulate the working day. By contrast, self-employed and lifestyle couriers are afforded no such protection; for these drivers, the payment system, linked to the number of successful deliveries, acts as a powerful force for compliance (Moore and Newsome, 2018; Newsome et al, 2018b).

These connections between contractual status and the exercise of management prerogative have been central to recent legal cases in the UK. Collective organization by workers who were assumed to be difficult to organize, both spatially and contractually, has started to challenge the model of self-employment. In the UK, improved conditions and changes to employment status have been gained through union negotiations and legal action by individual claimants. The GMB negotiated with courier service Hermes for improved conditions for self-employed couriers, including holiday pay (GMB, 2019), a fund to support couriers self-isolating due to COVID-19 (GMB, 2020) and increased payments (GMB, 2021a).

Several court cases have seen claimants successfully argue to be considered as workers rather than self-employed. *Dewhurst v CitySprint* (ET/220512/ 2016) saw a CitySprint bicycle courier win the right to holiday pay in line with what is afforded to those with worker status, while in the case of *Pimlico Plumbers v Smith*,[1] the judgment concluded that the claimant was a worker rather than an independent contractor. The concept of workers' preference for flexibility was central to Uber's unsuccessful attempt in October 2018 to overturn the Employment Tribunal decision (*Uber BV v Aslam*[2]) that confirmed drivers' status as workers. The company stated that defining drivers as workers could deprive them of the 'personal flexibility they value'[3] – the preference of the Uber drivers taking the case through an independent trade union was for workers' rights. In 2021, The Supreme Court upheld the decision in favour of the claimants for the right to be considered as workers rather than self-employed and hence to be entitled to the National Minimum Wage, pensions and holiday pay (*Uber BV and Ors v Aslam and Ors*[4]). Deon (2020) highlights that a key factor in all of these cases was the level of control companies had over claimants' work, as well as ratings and performance management in the case of Uber.

The ruling in favour of the claimants in the *Uber v Aslam* case was heralded as a win for Uber drivers, with potential ramifications for the broader gig economy. While the case will contribute to legal precedents for future tribunals and does represent positive progress in gaining rights for gig workers, it also highlights the inadequacy of the current legal framework. Uber was under no obligation to reclassify all of their drivers. Under the current UK legal framework, each driver would have to bring their own claims to access workers' rights (Deon, 2020). In their initial response, Uber highlighted that 'the UK Supreme Court ruled that a small group of *drivers* using the Uber app in 2016 should be classified as workers' (Uber UK, 2021: emphasis added). However, Uber did ultimately agree to afford holiday time, pension plans and the National Minimum Wage to their drivers, though National Minimum Wage payments would not apply to 'waiting time', where drivers are logged in to the app but waiting for jobs (GMB, 2021b).

Not all claims have been upheld in the courts. The Independent Workers Union of Great Britain sought statutory recognition to represent Deliveroo drivers from 2017 (*The Guardian*, 2021). However, it was unable to do so on the grounds that Deliveroo drivers were deemed independent contractors rather than workers. A key aspect of the decision in this case was that Deliveroo drivers were able to appoint a substitute to fulfil the work. In 2021, the Court of Appeal upheld previous rulings that Deliveroo drivers should be regarded as self-employed. This outcome gives further indication of how current legislation is not fit for purpose. The Taylor Review (Taylor et al, 2017: 36) spotlighted how the right to a substitute should not be 'an automatic barrier to accessing basic employment rights' and should not provide an easy way for companies to avoid responsibilities where, to all intents and purposes, the work 'looks and feels like employment'.

Conclusion

The invasive and controlling effects of digital technologies in modern work systems are rudely exposed in the differentiation of contractual forms in parcel delivery. It has been shown that in the absence of collective regulation, bogus self-employed parcel-delivery workers experience detailed surveillance and control that dictates pace, rhythm and piece-rate payment. Where, however, collective regulatory machinery has endured, the effort–reward nexus remains part of a negotiated order. The balance between unilateral control and negotiated outcomes may well shift as collective agency is asserted, either through legal challenges or worker organization. Indeed, this assertion may be reflected in the decline of self-employment since COVID-19.

This chapter has also problematized the notion of preference and autonomy in flexible work, in this case, self-employment. Organizational control over work, facilitated by digital technology, undermines the autonomy historically associated with self-employment. The availability of labour on an unpaid or paid basis reflects the predominance of one-sided flexibility and the asymmetry of power between employers and workers that the Taylor Review's notion of preference downplays. Behring and Harvey (2015: 971) have described the 'instituted economic process' that underpins the proliferation of 'self-employment', with legal, fiscal and economic processes co-constitutive of the labour market within which employment status is defined. Pollert's critique locates contractual differentiation within her broader analysis of the capital and labour dynamic, problematizing how far 'precarity' represents a qualitative or quantitative shift in capitalism.

As discussed, 'preference' over work is gendered, and self-employment may be more associated with male workers, reinforcing racial and ethnic networks, than other non-standard contracts, with zero- and minimum-hours more used by women and younger workers. Despite reference to the possibility that flexible work provides 'routes to progress in work' for those on lower incomes (Taylor et al, 2017: 6), evidence reveals that flexible workers are significantly more likely to find themselves out of work than those with a permanent contract (Heyes et al, 2018). Labour market segregation and inequality is reinforced by jobs offering no training and career progression. Flexibility, as Pollert asserted, obfuscates long-standing divisions of labour based on race and gender.

More broadly, through exploring notions of flexibility and work autonomy, and focusing on the contradictory relationship between digital technology and self-employment, this chapter has highlighted important issues that require further investigation. Why do workers on non-standard contracts, for example, home-care workers on zero-hours contracts, resist the offer of guaranteed-hours contracts? Why, following industrial action by Deliveroo workers, did a significant proportion reject the option of employment contracts and opt to remain 'self-employed'? What forms of workplace regulation and collective organization may shift the balance towards securing employment rights and autonomy over working time, and away from the further degradation of work through greater surveillance and monitoring?

Notes

[1] *Pimlico Plumbers Ltd & Anor v Smith* [2018] 4 All ER 641, [2018] WLR(D) 357, [2018] ICR 1511, [2018] UKSC 29, [2018] IRLR 872. Available at: www.bailii.org/uk/cases/UKSC/2018/29.html

[2] *Uber BV v Aslam* [2018] [2019] 3 All ER 489, [2019] RTR 25, [2019] IRLR 257, [2018] EWCA Civ 2748, [2019] WLR(D) 6, [2019] ICR 845. Available at: www.bailii.org/ew/cases/EWCA/Civ/2018/2748.html

[3] See: www.theguardian.com/technology/2018/dec/19/uber-loses-appeal-over-driver-employment-rights and www.theguardian.com/technology/2018/oct/30/uber-challenges-ruling-on-drivers-rights-at-court-of-appeal-london

[4] *Uber BV and Ors v Aslam and Ors* [2021] UKSC 5, [2021] WLR(D) 108. Available at: www.bailii.org/uk/cases/UKSC/2021/5.html

References

Bastani, A. (2019) *Fully Automated Luxury Communism: A Manifesto*, London: Verso.

Behling, F. and Harvey, M. (2015) 'The evolution of false self-employment in the British construction industry: a neo-Polanyian account of labour market formation', *Work, Employment and Society*, 29(6): 969–88.

Collier, R., Dubal, V. and Carter, C. (2017) 'Labor platforms and gig work: the failure to regulate', IRLE Working Paper No. 106–17, UC Hastings Research Paper No. 251. Available at: https://ssrn.com/abstract=3039742

Cowen, D. (2014) *The Deadly Life of Logistics: Mapping Violence in Global Trade*, Minneapolis, MN: University of Minnesota Press.

Deon, L. (2020) 'Regulating the scope of employment in the gig economy: towards enhanced rights at work in the age of Uber', *LSE Law Review*, 5: 190–208.

GMB (2019) 'Hermes and GMB in groundbreaking gig economy deal', GMB.

GMB (2020) 'Hermes pledge £1 million to help couriers self isolate', GMB.

GMB (2021a) 'GMB and Hermes agree further benefits for self employed plus couriers', GMB.

GMB (2021b) 'Uber "finally does the right thing" after GMB wins four court battles', GMB.

Gregory, K. (2021) '"My life is more valuable than this": understanding risk among on-demand food couriers in Edinburgh', *Work, Employment and Society*, 35(2): 316–31.

Gregson, N. (2017) 'Logistics at work: trucks, containers, and the friction of circulation in the UK', *Mobilities*, 12(3): 343–64.

Griesbach, K., Reich, A., Elliott-Negri, L. and Milkman, R. (2019) 'Algorithmic control in platform food delivery work', *Socius: Sociological Research for a Dynamic World*, 5: 1–15.

The Guardian (2021) 'Deliveroo riders suffer setback in court battle for right to unionise', *The Guardian*, 24 June.

Harvey, G., Rhodes, C., Vachhani, S. and Williams, K. (2017) 'Neo-villeiny and the service sector: the case of hyper flexible and precarious work in fitness centres', *Work, Employment and Society*, 31(1): 19–35.

Heyes, J., Moore, S., Newsome, K. and Tomlinson, M. (2018) 'Living with uncertain work', *Industrial Relations Journal*, 49(5–6): 420–37.

IFOW (Institute for the Future of Work) (2021) *The Amazonian Era: How Algorithmic Systems Are Eroding Good Work*, London: IFOW.

Josserand, E. and Kaine, S. (2019) 'Different directions or the same route? The varied identities of ride-share drivers', *Journal of Industrial Relations*, 61(4): 549–73.

Lloyd, C. and Payne, J. (2021) 'Fewer jobs, better jobs? An international comparative study of robots and "routine" work in the public sector', *Industrial Relations Journal*, 52(2): 109–24.

Low Pay Commission (2018) *A Response to Government on 'One-Sided Flexibility'*, London: LPC.

Mason, P. (2015) *Postcapitalism: A Guide to Our Future*, London: Allen Lane.

Moore, S. and Newsome, K. (2018) 'Paying for free delivery: self-employment in parcel delivery', *Work, Employment and Society*, 32(3): 475–92.

Moore, S., Antunes, B., Tailby, S. and Newsome, K. (2017) *Non-standard Contracts and the National Living Wage: A Report for the Low Pay Commission*, London: LPC.

Moore, S., Antunes, B., Tailby, S. and Newsome, K. (2018) '"Fits and fancies": the Taylor Review, the construction of preference and labour market segmentation', *Industrial Relations Journal*, 49(5–6): 403–19.

Moore, S. and Newsome, K. (2018) 'Paying for free delivery: self-employment in parcel delivery' *Work, Employment and Society* 32(3), 475–492

Newsome, K. (2015) 'Value in motion: logistics, labour and contemporary political economy', in K. Newsome, P. Taylor, A. Rainnie and J. Bair (eds) *The Missing Link: Integrating Labour with Global Value Chains*, Basingstoke: Palgrave Macmillan, pp 29–44.

Newsome, K., Heyes, J., Moore, S., Smith, D. and Tomlinson, M. (2018a) *Living on the Edge: The Experiences of Insecure Work in the UK*, London: TUC.

Newsome, K., Moore, S. and Ross, C. (2018b) '"Supply chain capitalism": exploring job quality for delivery workers in the UK', in T. Isidorsson and J. Kubisa (eds) *Job Quality in an Era of Flexibility: Experiences in a European Context*, London: Routledge, pp 81–98.

ONS (Office for National Statistics) (2020) 'Coronavirus and self-employment in the UK '. Available at: www.ons.gov.uk/employmentandlabourmarket/peopleinwork/employmentandemployeetypes/articles/coronavirusandselfemploymentintheuk/2020-04-24

ONS (2021a) 'LFS: self-employed: UK: all: 000s: SA: annual = 4 quarter average'. Available at: www.ons.gov.uk/employmentandlabourmarket/peopleinwork/employmentandemployeetypes/timeseries/mgrq/lms

ONS (2021b) 'Employment in the UK: April 2021'. Available at: www.ons.gov.uk/employmentandlabourmarket/peopleinwork/employmentandemployeetypes/bulletins/employmentintheuk/april2021

ONS (2021c) 'EMP14: employees and self-employed by industry EMP14'. Available at: https://www.ons.gov.uk/employmentandlabourmarket/peopleinwork/employmentandemployeetypes/datasets/employeesandselfemployedbyindustryemp14

ONS (2021d) 'Deaths involving coronavirus (COVID-19) by occupation (those aged 20 to 64 years), England and Wales: deaths registered between 9th March and 28th December 2020, coronavirus (COVID-19) related deaths by occupation, England and Wales'. Available at: www.ons.gov.uk/peoplepopulationandcommunity/healthandsocialcare/causesofdeath/bulletins/coronaviruscovid19relateddeathsbyoccupationenglandandwales/deathsregisteredbetween9marchand28december2020

Pollert, A. (1988) 'The "flexible firm": fixation or fact?', *Work, Employment and Society*, 2(3): 281–316.

Ravenelle, A.J. (2019) *Hustle and Gig: Struggling and Surviving in the Sharing Economy*, Berkeley, CA: University of California Press.

Rosenblat, A. (2018) *Uberland: How Algorithms Are Rewriting the World of Work*, Berkeley, CA: University of California Press.

Sowers, E.A. (2017) 'Logistics labor: insights from the sociologies of globalization, the economy, and work', *Sociology Compass*, 11(3): e12459.

Sun, P., Chen, J.Y. and Rani, U. (2023) 'From flexible labour to "sticky labour": a tracking study of workers in the food-delivery platform economy of China', *Work, Employment and Society*, 37(2): 412–31.

Taylor, M., Marsh, G., Nicol, D. and Broadbent, P. (2017) 'Good work: the Taylor Review of modern working practices', Department for Business, Energy & Industrial Strategy. Available at: www.gov.uk/government/uplo ads/system/uploads/attachment_data/file/627671/good-work-taylor-rev iew-modern-working-practices-rg.pdf

Uber UK (2021) 'Uber Blog, 19 February 2021: an update on Uber's Supreme Court verdict'. Available at: www.uber.com/en-GB/blog/supr eme-court-verdict/

12

Intersectionality and Industrial Relations

Anne McBride and Jenny K. Rodriguez[1]

Introduction

The celebration of 70 years of the British Universities Industrial Relations Association (BUIRA) is an apt time to consider contemporary challenges and discussions within industrial relations (IR), and this chapter is a contribution to those discussions. More specifically, it examines the relationship between intersectionality and IR, which continues to be ambiguous, undefined and full of tensions. At the same time, it is full of conceptual, theoretical, methodological and empirical possibilities. In 2006 and 2015, Holgate et al (2006) and McBride et al (2015), respectively, challenged us to pay more attention to gender, difference and intersectionality in the field of work and employment relations. More recently, Heery (2016: 171, 197) has noted that engagement with the gendered nature of the employment relationship is one of the most 'noticeable changes in writing about work and employment in recent times', with intersectionality 'currently the hottest concept within critical writing on equality and diversity'. This chapter is an attempt to more critically examine the use of the concept of intersectionality within IR and engage with the recent call by Lee and Tapia (2021: 1) for the 'incorporation of critical race and intersectional theory into IR to address the erasure of vital counter-narratives and to expand our empirical cases for labor and employment research'.

Within the confines of this short chapter, and inspired by Edward Said's (1983) idea of a travelling theory and Salem's (2018) application of it in relation to intersectionality, we explore how intersectionality, as grounded in discussions within feminist critical race theory, has been treated in IR scholarship. We develop our arguments from the reading of approximately

30 articles published in IR and IR-associated journals using the terms 'intersectional' and 'intersectionality'.[2] While this continues to be 'work in progress', we identify three trends from this initial scoping of such texts and a spectrum of usage. This ranges from the symbolic – where the term 'intersectionality' justifies the study of a more representative sample of workers, with no reference to its origins in critical race theory – through to those articles that actively engage with the concept as a means of using critical race theory to raise challenging questions for IR scholarship. We recognize the discussion of labour issues in other journals and return to a consideration of these work-related studies appearing outside of IR.[3]

This initial exploration enables us to note that while intersectionality remains largely underdeveloped in IR, there are signs that the term and its meaning have entered, albeit shyly, into discussions about contemporary IR. However, there are at least two departure points in this relationship that need further discussion. First, the detachment of intersectionality from its origins in critical race theory 'as a stand-alone concept' (Lee and Tapia, 2021: 8) undermines and depoliticizes the concept (Collins, 2000), and leads to it becoming a 'tool for *claiming* to attend to diversity, whilst subtly disguising the racist and classist inequalities which continue to exist between women' (Murphy, 2017: 14, emphasis in original; see also Salem, 2018). Second, the framing of intersectionality within critical race theory is an exciting challenge for us to rethink the tenets of IR that have shaped the study of employment relations hitherto (Lee and Tapia, 2021). Following a brief introduction to the concept of intersectionality, this chapter provides a critical appraisal of the use of intersectionality in IR scholarship before picking up on Lee and Tapia's (2021) challenge. The chapter concludes by posing some questions for IR scholars.

The roots of intersectionality

Intersectionality refers to the strength of interlocked systems of oppression that emerge from the simultaneous interaction of social categories of difference – such as gender, race, class, age, sexual orientation, disability and religion, among others – and create, establish and perpetuate dynamics of power that result in privilege and disadvantage (Crenshaw, 1989; Acker, 2006, 2012). Haslanger (2014: 116) identifies two questions central to intersectional thinking: (1) 'How does social categorization work and … how do social categories interact?'; and (2) 'How does power work and, more specifically, how do multiple axes of power interact to create structures of subordination?' These questions are related to the premise that experiences are multidimensional because of different modes of domination and power that result from the simultaneous interaction of social categories of difference and the privilege and disadvantage attached to them. In intersectional terms, these interactions are structurally embedded within all domains of life and work, so to understand the relationship between systems of power, inequality and oppression, as well as their causes and consequences, we must scrutinize the features that characterize the simultaneous intersection of social categories of difference and how these result in locations of privilege and disadvantage for specific groups.

The roots of intersectionality are linked to discussions that sought to grapple with the complexities of the experiences of exclusion faced by Black women and women of colour. On the one hand, the women's movement has historically been dominated by the interests of white women; on the other, the movements for racial equality and justice failed to consider the role of gender in the structural inequality and injustice affecting Black women and women of colour. The idea of intersectionality developed on the back of a history of activism that can be traced back to 'The Combahee River Collective statement' (The Combahee River Collective, 1977), where they noted:

> The most general statement of our politics at the present time would be that we are actively committed to struggling against racial, sexual, heterosexual, and class oppression, and see as our particular task the development of integrated analysis and practice based upon the fact that the major systems of oppression are interlocking. The synthesis of these oppressions creates the conditions of our lives.

This 'particular task' found its academic home in critical race theory, developed by legal scholars who studied the racialization of identity, racial subordination and the construction of race in legal texts, and scrutinized their application and the interpretation of the law in dealing with instances of discrimination and injustice (see Crenshaw et al, 1995). It was in the law discipline that intersectionality as a theory was coined; in her foundational article, 'Demarginalizing the intersection of race and sex: a black feminist critique of antidiscrimination doctrine, feminist theory and antiracist politics', legal scholar Kimberlé Crenshaw (1989: 139) problematized what she saw as 'the tendency [in antidiscrimination law, feminist theory and antiracist politics] to treat race and gender as mutually exclusive categories of experience and analysis'. In this article, she interrogated the framing, analysis and interpretation of the experiences of Black women who filed claims in courts in the US under Title VII of the Civil Rights Act 1964, which makes it illegal for employers to discriminate on the basis of race, colour, religion, sex and national origin. This led Crenshaw to conceptualize (as depicted in Table 12.1 later) structural, political and representational forms of intersectionality that create disadvantage and/or privilege through a matrix of domination (see also Collins, 2000).

The positioning within critical race theory took a further step in the discussion as a counterargument and radical critique of these forms of ontological exclusion by centring race as a key category even if not devoid of its own epistemological tensions on what explains anti–Black prejudice. For example, Delgado and Stefancic (2017: 21) note that there are divides between critical race theory thinkers; the authors recognize 'idealists', who consider racism and discrimination as 'matters of thinking, mental categorisation, attitude and discourse', and 'realists' who see it as the structural articulation of racial hierarchies as 'a means by which society allocates privilege and status'. This tension adds to the theoretical, methodological and empirical complexity of intersectionality, and is important in terms of how intersectionality has travelled within academic fields, including IR.

Intersectionality as a travelling theory: some evidence of the use of intersectionality in IR

The idea of travelling theory was put forward by Edward Said (1983) to allude to the potential of theories to alter as they move across disciplinary and regional boundaries. The potential of intersectionality to travel across disciplines has been discussed (see Rodriguez et al, 2016; Salem, 2018; Dias-Abey, 2022) to interrogate its theoretical, methodological and analytical value in engaging with a more nuanced way to understand systems of power, privilege, disadvantage and oppression. As with any travelling theory, attention must be placed on the tensions that are created by the reconfiguration of terminology to adjust it between disciplines (Salem, 2018). Both IR and intersectionality have inequality and its eradication at the heart of inquiry; in this respect, we see the use of an intersectional lens and a more explicit focus on interlocked forms of oppression that centre race as opportunities for IR to both refine the way it explores inequalities and broaden its analytical scope.

As noted earlier, there has been some engagement from IR scholars with intersectionality. We see evidence that intersectionality has travelled through the field and would argue that there is more untapped potential for this to be developed so that intersectionality is used more widely to engage with the critical questions that matter to IR scholarship that intersectionality can help to explore. However, we also need to be mindful that 'intersectionality neither travels outside nor is unmediated by the very field of race and gender power that it interrogates' (Cho et al, 2013: 791), as well as how the historical suppression of Black women's ideas has involved forms of incorporation and change that have depoliticized Black feminist ideas (Collins, 2000: 148; see also Lee and Tapia, 2021). Thus, although all of our examples focus on how the authors are using the concept to identify difference and study different experiences, a critical appraisal of the journey of intersectionality within

IR scholarship requires both the presentation and interrogation of its usage, for example, the lack of centrality of race, the lack of the problematization of whiteness and, more broadly, the risk of engaging in 'ornamental intersectionality' (see Bilge, 2013), which addresses diversity but does not address power structures or sustained injustices. The space constraints of this chapter only allow a few illustrative examples to be provided for each of the trends we identify, yet it enables two main critiques to be highlighted: how the concept of intersectionality is detached from critical race theory in the IR discipline; and the implications of that detachment.

Trend 1: Providing a nudge to intersectionality

This trend refers to those articles where authors are taking an 'intersectionally sensitive' approach (often citing McCall [2005] or McBride et al [2015]) to justify data collection from a more diverse sample of participants in categorical terms. These works answer calls by Wajcman (2000), Holgate et al (2006) and Rubery and Hebson (2018) to apply a gender lens and highlight what might otherwise be missing voices and experiences within the group of women. However, a lack of engagement with interlocking systems of oppression and the centrality of race in their reproduction and perpetuation means that the focus is on diversity, not intersectionality. This risks making the use of intersectionality appear superficial and 'neutralizing the critical potential of intersectionality for social justice-oriented change' (Bilge, 2013: 405).

Here, we examine the extent to which McBride et al's (2015) desire to make the concept more accessible has prompted a signalling, presentational effect rather than a fundamental change in thinking and analysis. Indeed, we must consider whether being intersectionality sensitive and making difference more visible is a sufficient, and appropriate, use of the concept of intersectionality in IR. Although McBride et al (2015) positioned the origins of intersectionality within critical race feminism, they did not fully engage with the idea of structural intersectionality that Crenshaw (1991) uses to frame how power dynamics marginalize Black women, and they did not reflect on their own racial identity when interpreting the concept. Instead, they used Crenshaw's concept of intersectionality to encourage all readers to be more aware of, and sensitive to, the diversity within groups (for example, of women). Only those interested in taking an 'intersectional approach' were encouraged to think more deeply about exploring systems of domination and discrimination, and the opportunity was missed to explicitly reflect on the role of whiteness and white privilege in systems of domination (McBride et al, 2015: 338).

This exploration of the journey of intersectionality in IR therefore suggests that while McBride et al (2015) encouraged greater engagement with the concept and provided a language and a justification for studying difference, their re-presentation of the concept of intersectionality may have led to the term becoming 'watered down' (Murphy, 2017: 14) and used primarily to discuss intersections of identity rather than of structural power (for critiques of its use in feminist theory, see Salem, 2018). Likewise, Cho et al (2013) acknowledge that the earlier work of McCall (2005) may have 'inadvertently fostered' an emphasis on overlapping identities rather than structures of power and exclusion. By justifying the need for intersectionality, these articles are attracting attention (as a nudge does) to the potential of this concept, though arguably in a way that fits Carbado's (2013) conception of 'colorblind intersectionality'. If we followed Hancock (2007), we could argue that articles written within this trend are applying a 'multiple' approach to difference rather than an intersectional approach.

Trend 2: Reporting the experiences of women of colour

This trend refers to articles that reference and engage with the Black feminist origins of intersectionality to explicitly justify the study of intersectional differences for women of colour and make them visible, such as Kaine's (2017) analysis of secondary data to show the labour market experiences of Aboriginal and Torres Strait Islander women. Likewise, Zuccotti and O'Reilly (2019) examine the differential effects of ethnicity, gender and parental households' employment status on young people not being in employment, education or training. Pringle et al (2017) build on Rodriguez et al (2016) to highlight the intersectional (pay) experiences of women engineers and care workers, as well as the advantages and disadvantages of immigrant status and being of the dominant ethnicity. In these cases, the theory has travelled to a place in IR where Black feminist thinking is used to support capturing differences arising from intersections of racio-ethnicity and other social categories of difference.

Despite a grounding in critical race feminism, an important question in this trend is whether it is sufficient to primarily use intersectionality to identify difference(s) either within or between groups. In their discussion about knowledge production in intersectionality studies, Cho et al (2013: 788) reject being 'preoccupied with "difference"' as an apt description of intersectionality's starting point; indeed, recognizing intersecting categories that shape experiences must be accompanied by an interrogation of how the multiple identities created by the intersections are invoked by and for individuals, and used to position them in locations that marginalize them as part of structures of power and domination.

Thinking about how intersectionality would travel to this point in IR, an avenue forward would be to engage more intentionally in adopting an intersectional lens to understand dynamics of privilege and disadvantage that sustain structural inequality in the workplace. Thus, the potential here is to take intersectionality's invitation to 'think from "both/and" spaces and to seek justice in crosscutting ways by identifying and addressing the (often hidden) workings of privilege and oppression' (May, 2015: 21).

Trend 3: Interrogating intersectionality

Work within this trend is distinguished by providing a means of analysing *how* structures of power marginalize and sustain inequality, and stand in contrast to previously discussed approaches that use intersectionality to identify the *who* and the *what*. There are fewer works that exemplify this trend within IR scholarship, and they often explain how multiple axes of power interact to create structures of subordination and how workers collectivize, resist and challenge their disadvantage. Notable examples include: Pearson et al's (2010) exploration of how the intersection of class, gender and ethnicity produced different, though also similar, experiences and forms of resistance for South Asian women in two UK workplaces in the 1970s and 2000s; Tapia et al's (2017: 487) discussion of how two US social movements intentionally focus and organize low-wage workers 'holding multiple identities in an increasingly diverse workforce'; Miles et al's (2019) interrogation of how the interrelating discriminations and intersectional experiences of women migrant workers in Malaysia raise specific challenges for advocacy group organizers; and Lee and Tapia's (2023) exploration of the dynamics of intersectional organizing, focusing on the 2017 US Women's March.

Other examples that we would place within the IR tradition are the work by Netto et al (2018), who examine the interaction of patriarchy within the home with racism and other structuring forces within the workplace, and the work of Bernardino-Costa (2014), who uses intersectionality to problematize the production of democratic mobilization, focusing on domestic workers' unions in Brazil. These latter two works, while discussing IR issues, are not published in IR journals.

Moving forward

This piece has highlighted that while intersectionality is not absent from scholarship about work and employment, there are important considerations in relation to depth, treatment and insight in its use. The primary question of why there is limited use of intersectionality within IR journals is complex and falls outside the remit of this short chapter; however, we recognize that the interrogation of patriarchy, sexism, racism and ableism, among others, and their relationship with work and employment are fundamental issues that should be taken up more comprehensively in IR scholarship to move away from theorization that has historically reflected heteronormative masculine priorities and privilege (Wajcman, 2000; Healy et al, 2006). Furthermore, we acknowledge porosity in disciplinary dialogue, which is impacted by works in this area being primarily published in journals focused on gender, race and ethnicity, disability, or equalities rather than IR journals.

Intersectionality presents many opportunities for theory and research in IR. Alongside Lee and Tapia (2021), we recognize broader arguments about the need to reframe the field's underlying theoretical assumptions. It is important, for example, to recognize the potential of intersectionality as a means to critically interrogate what shapes labour divisions and perceptions emerging within current models of capitalist accumulation, and doing so in ways that move beyond dichotomous positioning found in traditional class analysis and discussions about gender (de los Reyes, 2017). Drawing on Cho et al's (2013) proposed ways in which engagement with intersectionality can take place, its potential to advance discussions in IR lies in using it as a framework to investigate intersectional dynamics that shape systems of power, privilege, disadvantage and oppression in employment relations, and how this knowledge can inform and shape interventions (by employers, by unions, by policy makers and by governments) to address them.

Despite this potential, this does not come without critiques. Some (see Rubery and Hebson, 2018; Thornley and Coffey, 2011, cited in Heery, 2016: 197) have raised concerns that in decentring gender as a main analytical category, intersectionality risks marginalizing gender and taking discussion back to a gender-neutral approach, which echoes white feminist critiques of intersectionality. However, some (see Salem, 2018: 412) argue that there is a neoliberal intention to undermine and dilute intersectionality's strength as a strategy of resistance to create inclusive models of social justice, and instead turn it into a neoliberal approach that erases structural inequalities.

The argument that intersectionality risks breaking gender apart overlooks that most theorization about gender has been dominated by white feminists and has not fully engaged with the impact of race because this has not been central to the experiences of inequality of white women as a group. The implications of this are related not only to essentializing women as a group but also to the perpetuation of binary thinking, which is exclusive and myopic – class struggles, as well as gender relations, are racialized. Lee and Tapia (2021: 13) encourage IR scholars to 'form diverse and inclusive research teams'; we would add that attention should also be placed on race as a universal category of interrogation, not just one that focuses on 'difference' and 'otherness'. Instead, looking at racial privilege should also be part of the way we explore power relations and interlocked systems of oppression.

Another important tension is related to the perceived potential for intersectionality to dismantle notions of the collective that are fundamental to the definition of workers' interests, a tension that has been linked to an 'inevitable tendency to prioritise some inequalities over others' (Rubery and Hebson,

2018: 422). Using 'the collective' as a starting point of any such discussion assumes a generalized form of collective homogeneity, whereas using 'a collective' recognizes diverse group experiences. This is central to interrogating privilege and disadvantage, and while it remains an unresolved matter, some debates in IR (for example, the failure of union renewal agendas to attract diverse groups, and the proliferation of Black self-organizing within unions) signal the need to discuss more explicitly divisions and competing agendas in order to understand what shapes diverse experiences of work and employment.

The potential offered by intersectionality to IR starts off with a step back that recognizes differences in the experiences of work and employment of minoritized/marginalized groups, especially Black people and people of colour, and interrogates how intersections of race with other social categories of difference shape those experiences and the role of structures in perpetuating them. Some use intersectionality as a theory, others as a construct or heuristic device, and others as an analytical framework (Rodriguez et al, 2016). As a theory, intersectionality provides an epistemological standpoint where the departure is understanding identity as racialized and composed of multiple social categories of difference that overlap and intersect, and that operate simultaneously, are mobilized agentically and are invoked strategically.

As a heuristic device, it is a method used to detect overlapping and co-constructed strands of inequality by capturing and scrutinizing how intersections shape moments and events (Lutz, 2015; Raghuram, 2019). Crenshaw (1991: 1246) frames intersectionality as method as having a focus on understanding 'where systems of race, gender, and class discrimination converge'.

As an analytical framework, intersectionality takes into account different power contexts to identify both visible and not-so-visible factors that structurally shape experiences of disadvantage and marginalization. Anthias (1998) has proposed a multi-level analysis that focuses on four dimensions: experiences of discrimination (individual), intersubjective praxis (group), institutional regimes (institutions) and the symbolic and discursive (representations). In Table 12.1, we present some considerations to help in engaging with an intersectional lens in IR.

Conclusion

The purpose of this chapter has been to reflect on how intersectionality has travelled through IR by identifying trends in its use in IR scholarship. The exploration has allowed us to reflect on issues that hint at the meaning and conceptual boundaries that shape the thinking and analysis of inequalities in the IR discipline. We identified three trends of engagement with intersectionality in the IR literature: first, works that give a nudge to intersectionality, naming it and using it to justify the use of different analytical categories; second, works that enable the gist of intersectionality

Table 12.1: Thinking intersectionally

Key questions	Operationalization	Some considerations for IR
How do we approach the intersection of social categories of difference?	Scholars consider how social categories of difference come together to create privilege and disadvantage. There are two approaches: • *Additive approach:* thinking about how individual categories add to the overall experiences of work and employment of particular groups. • *Multiplicative approach:* thinking about how the simultaneous intersection of categories shapes the overall experiences of work and employment of particular groups.	Consider the role of race/racio-ethnicity in power dynamics in the workplace/sector and how race/racio-ethnicity intersects with other social categories of difference. Consider how social categories of difference are relevant to the experiences of work and employment in discussion, and why. Consider how these social categories of difference intersect to shape those experiences of work and employment. Consider both the privilege and the disadvantage that these intersections produce/reproduce.
What can intersectionality help us to show?	Scholars decide on an approach based on what they want their work to highlight: • *Structural intersectionality:* focus on existing and routinized forms of domination that are part of social structures. • *Political intersectionality:* focus on exploring how and whether intersectionality is embedded in public policies. • *Representational intersectionality:* focus on the everyday (social and cultural constructions) of groups and how these shape institutions, structures and practices.	At the structural level, consider how intersections are articulated and mobilized in the workplace, and make groups of workers privileged or disadvantaged (for example, how narratives and practices about work and employment create and perpetuate privilege and disadvantage for groups located at the centre of an intersection). At the political level, consider how macro-level regimes (such as regulatory frameworks) position groups of workers based on how the frameworks impact them in disproportionate ways (either to create disadvantage or to create privilege). At the representational level, consider how intersections are linked with privilege and disadvantage experienced by groups of workers.
How do we operationalize and analyse the intersections between social categories of difference?	Scholars structure analysis to highlight categorical complexity and show instances where these are mobilized and invoked to shape experiences of groups. Three points of operationalization that help with intersectional analysis are: • focus on which categories are relevant; • focus on how categories are positioned within hierarchies of power; and • focus on commonalities across categories that lead to instances of disadvantage or privilege.	Consider how social categories of difference inform particular accounts from those involved (such as workers, unions and management). Consider what particular assumptions and narratives are produced and reproduced (due to presence or invisibility) in policies and practices. Consider patterns or representational trends in social categories of difference that could help to explain phenomena. Consider how social categories of difference interact to shape dimensions of the experiences of work and employment.

Source: Adapted from Rodriguez (2018)

and its importance to be identified, even if not fully developing intersectional analyses; and, third, works that adopt an intersectional lens to interrogate interlocking systems of oppression and how these create and perpetuate privilege and disadvantage.

These trends speak of different degrees of engagement, and while we are critical of their limitations, it is important to recognize their value in providing a much-needed starting point from which to continue using intersectionality in IR. To that effect, we provided some points of consideration and would argue that a key message is that intersectionality presents us with an opportunity to think about the IR field more broadly, not just as an alternative way to conduct IR studies. Implicit in discussions in this chapter is the importance of thinking more insightfully about the role of whiteness and white privilege in the production of knowledge within IR (Lee and Tapia, 2021).

Challenging hierarchies of power that disadvantage and oppress minoritized/marginalized groups is both about understanding what differential status of particular groups looks like and about interrogating what underpins the production and perpetuation of that status (for such reflection in the context of Aotearoa/New Zealand, see Murphy, 2017). In terms of research work, there are also questions of appropriateness and crafting linked to the adoption of intersectionality; the roots of the concept of intersectionality within critical race theory remind us to question the centrality of race/racio-ethnicity in how 'society allocates privilege and status' (Delgado and Stefancic, 2017: 17) and how it may be shaping privilege and disadvantage within (and outside) the workplace.

Finally, we recognize that the importance of adopting intersectionality was initially thought of to centre the systematic oppression experienced by Black women and women of colour as a marginalized/minoritized group in US society. Disciplinarily, the translation of these discussions into IR needs to consider situated structured relationships in power and group entitlements in the dynamics of work and employment, as well as how these are reconfigured in other settings and transnationally. For instance, hierarchies of power, privilege, disadvantage and oppression happen not only across racial differences (for example, Black women and women of colour in white-dominated settings) but also within more complex racio-ethnic frameworks, for example, where Black women and women of colour are not primarily living in white, Western societies (Yuval-Davis, 2011; see also Miles et al, 2019). In this respect, this chapter would also call for translation that does not essentialize privilege or disadvantage but focuses on engaging with the potential offered by intersectionality to scrutinize hierarchies of power that are of disciplinary importance to IR scholarship.

A good point on which to close this chapter is to reinforce our message by noting that the value of intersectionality in IR is that it helps in 'capturing the synergistic relation between inequalities as grounded in the lived experience of hierarchy [that changes] not only what people think about inequality but the way they think' (MacKinnon, 2013: 1028).

Notes

[1]   Authorship contributions are joint and equal.

[2]   Such journals include: *Journal of Industrial Relations; Industrial Relations Journal; British Journal of Industrial Relations; European Journal of Industrial Relations; International Journal of Comparative Labour Law and Industrial Relations; Economic and Industrial Democracy; Work, Employment and Society; Transfer; New Zealand Journal of Employment Relations; Industrial and Labor Relations Review;* and *International Journal of Human Resource Management.*

[3]   Such journals include: *Gender, Work and Organization; British Journal of Management; Equality, Diversity and Inclusion; Journal of World Business; Sex Roles; British Journal of Guidance & Counselling; Disability & Society;* and *Organization.*

References

Acker, J. (2006) 'Inequality regimes: gender, class, and race in organizations', *Gender & Society*, 20(4): 441–64.

Acker, J. (2012) 'Gendered organizations and intersectionality: problems and possibilities', *Equality, Diversity and Inclusion: An International Journal*, 31(3): 214–24.

Anthias, F. (1998) 'Rethinking social divisions: some notes towards a theoretical frame-work', *Sociological Review*, 46(3): 505–35.

Bernardino-Costa, J. (2014) 'Intersectionality and female domestic workers' unions in Brazil', *Women's Studies International Forum*, 46: 72–80.

Bilge, S. (2013) 'Intersectionality undone: saving intersectionality from feminist intersectionality studies', *Du Bois Review: Social Science Research on Race*, 10(2): 405–24.

Carbado, D.W. (2013) 'Colorblind intersectionality', *Signs: Journal of Women in Culture and Society*, 38(4): 811–45.

Cho, S., Crenshaw, K.W. and McCall, L. (2013) 'Toward a field of intersectionality studies: theory, applications, and praxis', *Signs: Journal of Women in Culture and Society*, 38(4): 785–810.

Collins, P.H. (2000) *Black Feminist Thought: Knowledge, Consciousness, and the Politics of Empowerment*, 2nd edn, New York: Routledge.

The Combahee River Collective (1977) 'The Combahee River Collective statement'. Available at: www.loc.gov/item/lcwaN0028151/

Crenshaw, K. (1989) 'Demarginalizing the intersection of race and sex: a black feminist critique of antidiscrimination doctrine, feminist theory and antiracist politics', *University of Chicago Legal Forum*, 1(8): 138–67.

Crenshaw, K. (1991) 'Race, gender, and sexual harassment', *Southern California Law Review*, 65: 1467–76.

Crenshaw, K., Gotanda, N., Peller, G. and Thomas, K. (eds) (1995) *Critical Race Theory: Key Writings That Formed the Movement*, New York: The New Press.

Delgado, R. and Stefancic, J (2017) *Critical Race Theory*, 3rd edn, New York: New York University Press.

De los Reyes, P. (2017) 'Working life inequalities: do we need intersectionality?', *Society, Health & Vulnerability*, 8(S1): 14–18.

Dias-Abey, M. (2022) 'Mobilizing for recognition: indie unions, migrant workers, and strategic Equality Act litigation', *International Journal of Comparative Labour Law and Industrial Relations*, 38(2): 137–56.

Hancock, A.-M. (2007) 'When multiplication doesn't equal quick addition: examining intersectionality as a research paradigm', *Perspectives on Politics*, 5(1): 63–79.

Haslanger, S. (2014) 'Race, intersectionality, and method: a reply to critics', *Philosophical Studies*, 171(1): 109–19.

Healy, G., Hansen, L.L. and Ledwith, S. (2006) 'Still uncovering gender in industrial relations', *Industrial Relations Journal*, 37(4): 290–8.

Heery, E. (2016) *Framing Work, Unitary, Pluralist and Critical Perspectives in the Twenty-First Century*, Oxford: Oxford University Press.

Holgate, J., Hebson, G. and McBride, A. (2006) 'Why gender and "difference" matters: a critical appraisal of industrial relations research', *Industrial Relations Journal*, 37(4): 310–28.

Kaine, S. (2017) 'Women, work and industrial relations in Australia in 2016', *Journal of Industrial Relations*, 59(3): 271–87.

Lee, T.L. and Tapia, M. (2021) 'Confronting race and other social identity erasures: the case for critical industrial relations theory', *ILR Review*, 74(3): 637–62.

Lee, T.L. and Tapia, M. (2023) 'Intersectional organizing: building solidarity through radical confrontation', *Industrial Relations: A Journal of Economy and Society*, 62(1): 78–111.

Lutz, H. (2015) 'Intersectionality as method', *DiGeSt. Journal of Diversity and Gender Studies*, 2(1–2): 39–44.

MacKinnon, C.A. (2013) 'Intersectionality as method: a note', *Signs: Journal of Women in Culture and Society*, 38(4): 1019–30.

May, V.M. (2015) *Pursuing Intersectionality, Unsettling Dominant Imaginaries*, New York: Routledge.

McBride, A., Hebson, G. and Holgate, J. (2015) 'Intersectionality: are we taking enough notice in the field of work and employment relations?', *Work, Employment and Society*, 29(2): 331–41.

McCall, L. (2005) 'The complexity of intersectionality', *Signs: Journal of Women in Culture and Society*, 30(3): 1771–800.

Miles, L., Lewis, S., Teng, L.W. and Yasin, S.M. (2019) 'Advocacy for women migrant workers in Malaysia through an intersectionality lens', *Journal of Industrial Relations*, 61(5): 682–703.

Murphy, L. (2017) 'Intersectional feminisms: reflections on theory and activism in Sarah Ahmed's *Living a Feminist Life*', *Women's Studies Journal*, 31(2): 4–17.

Netto, G., Noon, M., Hudson, M., Kamenou-Aigbekaen, N. and Sosenko, F. (2018) 'Intersectionality, identity work and migrant progression from low-paid work: a critical realist approach', *Gender, Work and Organization*, 27: 1020–38.

Pearson, R., Anitha, S. and McDowell, L. (2010) 'Striking issues: from labour process to industrial dispute at Grunwick and Gate Gourmet', *Industrial Relations Journal*, 41(5): 408–28.

Pringle, J., Davies, S., Giddings, L.S. and McGregor, J. (2017) 'Gender pay equity and wellbeing: an intersectional study of engineering and caring occupations', *New Zealand Journal of Employment Relations*, 42(3): 29–45.

Raghuram, P. (2019) 'Race and feminist care ethics: intersectionality as method', *Gender, Place and Culture: A Journal of Feminist Geography*, 26(5): 613–37.

Rodriguez, J.K., Holvino, E., Fletcher, J.K. and Nkomo, S.M. (2016) 'The theory and praxis of intersectionality in work and organisations: where do we go from here?', *Gender, Work and Organization*, 23(3): 201–21.

Rubery, J. and Hebson, G. (2018) 'Applying a gender lens to employment relations: revitalisation, resistance and risks', *Journal of Industrial Relations*, 60(3): 414–36.

Said, E. (1983) *The World, the Text, and the Critic*, Cambridge, MA: Harvard University Press.

Salem, S. (2018) 'Intersectionality and its discontents: intersectionality as traveling theory', *European Journal of Women's Studies*, 25(4): 403–18.

Tapia, M., Lee, T. and Filipovitch, M. (2017) 'Supra-union and intersectional organizing: an examination of two prominent cases in the low wage US restaurant industry', *Journal of Industrial Relations*, 59(4): 487–509.

Thornley, C. and Coffey, D. (2011) 'Model employment? The challenges ahead for public sector employers and unions in tackling the gender pay gap', in T. Wright and H. Conley (eds) *Gower Handbook of Discrimination at Work*, Farnham: Gower, pp 59–68.

Wajcman, J. (2000) 'Feminism facing industrial relations in Britain', *British Journal of Industrial Relations*, 38(2): 183–201.

Yuval-Davis, N. (2011) 'Beyond the recognition and re-distribution dichotomy: intersectionality and stratification', in H. Lutz, M.T. Herrera Vivar and L. Supik (eds) *Framing Intersectionality: Debates on a Multi-faceted Concept in Gender Studies*, Farnham: Ashgate, pp 155–69.

Zuccotti, C.V. and O'Reilly, J. (2019) 'Ethnicity, gender and household effects on becoming NEET: an intersectional analysis', *Work, Employment and Society*, 33(3): 351–73.

Index

References to endnotes show both the page number and the note number (22n1).